Cajun

Low-Carb

Other books
by Jude W. Theriot, CCP

Cajun Quick (1992)
La Meilleure de la Louisiane (1980)
New American Light Cuisine (1988)
La Cuisine Cajun (1990)
Cajun Healthy (1994)

Cajun
Low-Carb

Jude W. Theriot, CCP

PELICAN PUBLISHING COMPANY
Gretna 2005

*The word "Pelican" and the depiction of a pelican are trademarks
of Pelican Publishing Company, Inc., and are registered in the
U.S. Patent and Trademark Office.*

Library of Congress Cataloging-in-Publication Data

Theriot, Jude W.
  Cajun low-carb / Jude W. Theriot.
      p. cm.
  Includes index.
  ISBN 978-1-58980-264-3 (alk. paper)
  1. Cookery, American—Louisiana style. 2. Cookery, Cajun. 3. Low-
carbohydrate diet—Recipes. I. Title.

  TX715.2.L68T473 2005
  641.5'6383'09763—dc22

                                    2004022590

Printed in the United States of America
Published by Pelican Publishing Company, Inc.
1000 Burmaster Street, Gretna, Louisiana 70053

To my mother, Mary Louise Borel Theriot. Mom's passing was tough on all of us. She was a wonderful, loving, and caring mother, but she was also a genuine friend. She never had an ill word to say about anyone. She always pushed her children to be the best they could be, but always made us feel that she was proud of whatever we'd accomplished. Losing a loved one is hard to bear, but losing your mother is almost unbearable. Mom is always on my mind and in my heart. I know she would have loved this book and what it has already done for me and a number of my family members. Mom, this book is for you. I love you.

Contents

Introduction

Well, it's time for another book. It's really hard to believe this will be my sixth book! I really just set out to write one book, *La Meilleure de la Louisiane* (*The Best of Louisiana*). I thought that was the only book I had in me. Time proved that wrong. Times change—and with it people change, cooking styles change, and techniques change. As we evolve, we change what we cook and how we eat.

That's why I've written this book. I want to share with the reader what I've learned in my ongoing development as a cookbook writer and as a culinary professional.

It's hard to go anywhere today and not be impacted by the low-carb craze. But I've had to look beyond the craze. I wanted to find out how it would fit in my daily lifestyle and see if it offered any hope for me individually especially in the area of weight control. Those who know me know that I have battled my whole life with weight problems. The problem, of course, is mainly that I love to cook and I love to eat. I've tried every diet known to man and they've all worked, but only for a while.

Why did they fail? They failed because I couldn't stay with it. In order for diets to work, they have to change your lifestyle and have to offer you a new way to live, not just a new way to eat. I studied the low-carb diet for quite a while before I decided to give it a try. Now, after over a year, I can say that I will be able to stay on this diet for the rest of my life. Unlike with other diets, you don't have to completely change your lifestyle. You can still eat at your favorite restaurants. You don't have to pack snacks when you leave town, carry a book around everywhere, or feel restricted in where you can eat.

Dr. Atkins, the founder of the Atkin's diet, said that fat was not the enemy. The enemy was simple carbohydrates. Take pigs, for example. What do we feed them to make them fat? We feed them grain! Heavy, simple carbohydrates is the food of choice to fatten pigs. Yet many people claimed, especially during the 1980s, that a high-carb diet was the way to lose weight. "Stay away from fats" was the mantra of the day. Fats make you fat. It sounds right, but in reality carbohydrates are a major player in weight gain. Americans today are fatter than ever and we eat more carbs than ever. We saw a plunge in the amount of fats that the nation consumed, yet we got fatter. For some of us, fat is not the problem.

Consult a doctor before trying this or any other diet. Diets that may be great for one person can be harmful for another. The low-carb diet might not be right for you, but I do know that for me, this works! It is something I can stay with. I'm one of those people who is allergic to carbs. Carbs, even though they are lower in calories than fat, actually make me fat because my body doesn't process them the same way other people's do. Simple carbs make me produce glucose. That glucose causes my insulin level to spike, which makes me hungry and causes me to eat more. Of course, if I eat more carbs, the cycle continues and I end up storing more excess calories as fat.

How do I know that's true? I've charted it. I know that when I'm on a low-carb diet, I eat less and less. I get hungry less often. When I do get hungry, I know that eating a reasonable amount of high-protein food satiates my appetite. I feel fuller faster, so I avoid eating excess calories, which are stored as fat. Over time, I've seen a dramatic drop in how much I eat and how hungry I get.

That's it in a nutshell. With your doctor's approval, try these great-tasting, low-carb recipes for yourself. I know you won't be disappointed.

Net carbs is the difference between the total carb count and the amount of fiber and sugar alcohol in a serving. To get the net carb count, subtract the amount of fiber from the total carb count. The reason we can use the net carb value is simply because the body doesn't digest the fiber carbs and the sugar alcohol does not result in a rise in insulin production.

Sharing recipes is like sharing a part of yourself. Food is how we as a people celebrate almost everything. Food is close to our culture. We cook and eat what we like. That makes us unique and special. I hope *Cajun Low-Carb* helps you live a better life and enjoy it more. Remember while we do eat to live, a Cajun, even a low-carb Cajun, lives to eat! I hope this book helps as you change your eating habits to lose weight and gain that Cajun *joie de vie!*

Lagniappe

As has been the tradition of my cookbooks, I have included a *lagniappe* section on each recipe in this book. This section is to help the reader really get to know each of the recipes on a more personal note. I try to step out of the traditional directions and give you hints and ideas that will make cooking each recipe extra special and easier. It also contains general cooking tips, stories from Cajun history, from my own personal history or any interesting or informative information I can give you.

Lagniappe is a Cajun French word that means "a little something extra" or "a little something for nothing." In the olden days, proprietors of stores (or even roadside stands) would always throw in a little something with the purchase, just as a gesture of good will. It is somewhat similar to the "baker's dozen."

Today, the word has kept its meaning, but alas, the custom is almost gone. However, because I give you my lagniappe with each recipe, you get to experience just what the practice was like. These *lagniappe* sections are filled with hints, suggestions, ideas, cooking techniques, and things that will make the recipe easier. They might also contain bits of humor (at least as I see it). I'll tell you how to freeze leftovers and how to revive them the next day. I also included carb, net carb, and calorie counts.

When I considered dropping this section, I was overwhelmingly told that the *lagniappe* section was what made my books and recipes stand out and become uniquely personal. There are a lot of cookbook-buyers that like to read cookbooks the way some like to read novels. I guess that's good, especially for cookbook authors. This *lagniappe* section allows me to talk to the reader. I know I like it and I hope it adds to your enjoyment of the book. There are a lot of cookbooks out there and but not all of them offer anything more than recipes. So I offer this added value to you, by giving you a little something extra.

I hope you enjoy the *lagniappe* section and take advantage of the section while using the book. It will help make the experience of using *Cajun Low-Carb* one you enjoy, learn from, and maybe just find entertaining!

Note: For all recipes, carbohydrate and net carbohydrates are given in grams. The word "trace" indicates a negligible amount of carbohydrates for that recipe per serving. Calories are listed as a count for the serving listed in the recipe.

Cajun
Low-Carb

Seasoning Mixes

SEAFOOD SEASONING MIX

¼ cup salt
2 tbsp. cayenne pepper
1 tbsp. black pepper
1 tbsp. white pepper
2 tbsp. paprika
1½ tbsp. onion powder
1 tbsp. garlic powder
2 tsp. dried sweet basil

1 tsp. dried parsley
½ tsp. dry hot mustard
½ tsp. ground file powder
¼ tsp. dried thyme
¼ tsp. dried oregano
¼ tsp. dried tarragon
¼ tsp. dried rosemary
⅛ tsp. cloves

In a large mixing bowl, blend all the ingredients together well. Store in a tightly covered glass jar for use as needed. This is an excellent seasoning for all seafoods. Use this seasoning mix as you would use salt. Do not add additional salt to any dish using this seasoning mix. Makes about ½ cup of seasoning mix. Serving size is 1 tsp.

Lagniappe: This seasoning mix lends itself mainly to seafood but it is generally a good seasoning for any dish. You can make a large amount at one time and store for later use or give as gifts during the year or at Christmas time.

Carbs per serving: trace
Net Carbs per serving: trace
Calories per serving: 1

CHICKEN SEASONING MIX

¼ cup salt

3 tbsp. cayenne pepper

2 tbsp. black pepper

1 tbsp. white pepper

2 tbsp. paprika

2 tbsp. onion powder

1 tbsp. garlic powder

1 tbsp. dried sweet basil

2 tsp. dried parsley

2 tsp. dry hot mustard

½ tsp. ground file powder

1 tsp. dried rosemary

¼ tsp. dried thyme

¼ tsp. dried oregano

¼ tsp. dried marjoram

⅛ tsp. all spice

⅛ tsp. cloves

In a large mixing bowl, blend all the ingredients together well. Store in a tightly covered glass jar for use as needed. This is an excellent seasoning for all poultry. Use this seasoning mix as you would use salt. Do not add additional salt to any dish using this seasoning mix. Makes about ½ cup of seasoning mix. Serving size is 1 tsp.

Lagniappe: This seasoning mix lends itself mainly to poultry but it is generally a good seasoning for any dish. You can make a large amount at one time and store for later use or give as gifts during the year.

Carbs per serving: trace
Net Carbs per serving: trace
Calories per serving: 1

HOLLANDAISE SAUCE

6 egg yolks
2 tbsp. lemon juice, fresh squeezed
1 tbsp. water
1 tsp. Tabasco® Sauce
1 tsp. salt
½ tsp. white pepper
1 cup melted butter, warm

Add all the ingredients except for the butter to the top half of a double boiler and heat over low, stirring constantly with a wire whisk. When the sauce starts to thicken, slowly drizzle the butter into the pot until all the butter is used, stirring constantly. When the sauce thickens nicely, remove from the heat and store at room temperature until you are ready to serve. Do not store for longer than 1 hour. Makes about 2 cups of sauce. Serving size is 1 tsp.

Lagniappe: This sauce adds flavor and richness to almost any food. It is great on meats, seafood, chicken, or vegetables. You can cover tightly and store leftovers in the refrigerator. When you are ready to use, let stand at room temperature for 20 minutes, then beat the sauce with a wire whisk. For a little variety, you can add ½ teaspoon of cayenne pepper to the sauce to make a Hollandaise with a little bit of a kick!

Carbs per tablespoon: trace
Net Carbs per tablespoon: trace
Calories per tablespoon: 64

BÉARNAISE SAUCE

6 egg yolks
2 tbsp. lemon juice, fresh squeezed
1 tbsp. tarragon vinegar
1 tsp. Worcestershire sauce
1 tbsp. dry white wine
½ tbsp. tarragon leaves

1 tsp. Tabasco® Sauce
1 tsp. salt
½ tsp. white pepper
½ tsp. cayenne pepper
1 cup melted butter, warm

Add all the ingredients except for the butter to the top half of a double boiler and heat over low heat, stirring constantly with a wire whisk. When the sauce starts to thicken, slowly drizzle the butter into the pot until all the butter is used, stirring constantly. When the sauce thickens nicely, remove from the heat and store at room temperature until you are ready to serve. Do not store for longer than 1 hour. Makes about 2 cups of sauce.

Lagniappe: Béarnaise is almost a Hollandaise except for the tarragon leaves and tarragon vinegar. It's amazing how a simple change creates such a dramatic difference in taste, texture, and flavor. Béarnaise is wonderful on beef, chicken, and seafood. Be sure to store any leftovers in a tightly-covered bowl in the refrigerator. It can keep for up to 1 week. To serve, let it thaw at room temperature for 20 minutes, then whip it back to life with a wire whisk.

Carbs per tablespoon: trace
Net Carbs per tablespoon: trace
Calories per tablespoon: 62

LIGHT CREAM SAUCE

3 tbsp. unsalted butter
2 tbsp. soy flour
1 tbsp. all purpose flour
½ tsp. salt
1 tsp. Tabasco® Sauce

½ tsp. black pepper
½ cup half-and-half
½ cup heavy whipping cream
¼ cup of Chicken Stock (see p. 88) or
   chicken broth

In a medium saucepan over low heat, melt the butter. Slowly add the flour and soy flour, stirring constantly with a wire whisk. Cook for 3 minutes, stirring constantly. Add the salt, Tabasco® Sauce, and black pepper and stir in well. Slowly add the half-and-half, stirring constantly. The sauce may clump up a bit, but you can stir the lumps back into the sauce by whipping with the whisk. Add the heavy cream, stirring constantly. When the cream is used, slowly add the stock. Cook one minute then remove from the heat. Makes about 1 cup of sauce.

Lagniappe: This is a wonderful sauce to use as a base for other sauces. It can be used alone or as a light cream sauce on sauce chicken or pork dishes. You can add the shredded cheese of your choice to make wonderful cheese sauces. A little of this sauce added to the natural juices that cooking any meat creates makes a wonderful sauce as well.

Carbs per tablespoon: .9 g.
Net carbs per tablespoon: .7 g.
Calories per tablespoon: 37

BECHAMEL SAUCE

2 tbsp. salted butter
1 tbsp. soy flour
½ tbsp. all purpose flour
¾ cup half-and-half
½ tsp. salt

½ tsp. white pepper
½ tsp. Tabasco® Sauce
¼ tsp. fresh lemon juice
1 tbsp. onion, finely chopped

In a heavy saucepan over low heat, melt the butter. Stir in the soy flour and flour with a wire whisk taking care to make sure completely absorbed. Cook over low heat for 3 minutes. Add the half-and-half slowly, stirring constantly. Cook until the sauce thickens, then add the remaining ingredients. Stir in well and cook for 1 minute. Makes about ¾ cup of sauce.

Lagniappe. This is a sauce for flavoring meats and seafoods. It can also be used as a base to make other sauces. Take care that the clumps that may develop when you add the half-and-half are completely dissolved back into the sauce.

Carbs per tablespoon: .75 g.
Net carbs per tablespoon: .6 g.
Calories per tablespoon: 31

BORDELAISE SAUCE

½ cup unsalted butter
¼ cup extra virgin olive oil
3 cloves garlic, minced
1 tbsp. shallots, minced
2 tbsp. red bell pepper, finely diced
2 tbsp. green onion bottoms, finely minced

½ tsp. salt
1 tsp. fresh ground black pepper
1 tsp. Tabasco® Sauce
¼ cup dry red wine
¼ cup fresh parsley, minced
2 tbsp. Bechamel Sauce (see p. 27)

In a heavy, medium sized skillet over medium heat, add the butter and olive oil and let it get hot. Add the garlic, shallots, bell pepper, and green onions and sauté for 3 minutes, stirring constantly. Add the salt, pepper, and Tabasco® Sauce and blend in well. Raise the heat to high and when it begins to sizzle, add the red wine and parsley. Cook for 1minute, stirring constantly. Reduce the heat and add 2 tbsp. of Bechamel Sauce and blend until the sauce is smooth. Remove from the heat. Makes about 1 cup of sauce.

Lagniappe: This is a classic sauce that is really made from deglazing the pan with the red wine. Be sure to use a quality wine, because the sauce will carry the flavor of the wine you use. If you are serving a dinner wine, be sure to use the same wine to make the sauce. I generally like to recork and save unused wine to make my sauces. While the wine may not be good for drinking, it is great for sauce making.

Carbs per tablespoon: .7 g.
Net carbs per tablespoon: .6 g.
Calories per tablespoon: 67

BROWN SAUCE

2 tbsp. clarified unsalted butter
1 tbsp. all purpose flour
1 tbsp. soy flour
2 cups seafood stock, boiling
½ cup onion, chopped
1 tbsp. Worcestershire sauce
1 tbsp. tomato puree

1 bay leaf
¼ tsp. oregano
¼ tsp. garlic powder
½ tsp. cayenne pepper
1 tsp. salt
½ tsp. black pepper
2 tbsp. Burgundy wine

In a small saucepan over medium-high heat, heat the clarified butter until it is hot, then add the flour and soy flour all at once and blend in well. Stir constantly with a wire whisk, cooking for about 7 minutes or until the roux begins to brown. Remove from the heat and set aside. In a medium saucepan, add the boiling seafood stock add the remaining ingredients except for the wine and cook for 1½ hours over low simmering heat, stirring occasionally. Add the brown roux that you set aside to the simmering stock and blend it in well. Simmer this sauce over low heat for 30 more minutes, stirring occasionally. Remove from the heat and add the wine; mix in well. Makes about 1 cup of sauce.

Lagniappe: This is another classic sauce. It is seldom used alone; it is generally added to other sauces or dishes to enhance the flavor. You can completely make this in advance and refrigerate for later use. It sometimes helps to make the brown sauce one day and the final sauce a day or two later. I have frozen this sauce with fairly good success. Just let it thaw in the refrigerator and over low heat until the sauce is warm.

Carbs per tablespoon: 1.3 g.
Net carbs per tablespoon: 1 g.
Calories per tablespoon: 11

CAJUN LOW-CARB MEUNIERE SAUCE

1 cup Brown Sauce (see p. 28 for recipe) 2 tbsp. lemon juice, fresh
1 stick butter, cut into pats then quarters 1 tsp. Tabasco® Sauce
1 tbsp. Worcestershire sauce 2 tbsp. fresh parsley, minced

In a quart saucepan over medium heat, bring the Brown Sauce to a quick simmer. Add the butter, Worcestershire sauce and Tabasco® Sauce. Whip with a wire whisk until the butter is completely absorbed into the sauce. Add the lemon juice and parsley and whip again until the sauce is smooth. Remove from the heat. Sauce is to be used as soon as possible and should not be held for more than 30 minutes. Makes about 1¼ cup of sauce.

Lagniappe: This is an excellent sauce for almost any fish, crab, or shrimp dish. This is a sauce to please. It takes a little bit of time to make, but isn't time what great cooking is about? Great sauces take time, but the effort is worth the wait. Unfortunately, this sauce can't be kept for longer than 30 minutes, but the Brown Sauce can be made in advance and refrigerated until you are ready to use.

Carbs per tablespoon: 1.3 g.
Net carbs per tablespoon: 1.1 g.
Calories per tablespoon: 51

MARCHAND DE VIN SAUCE

½ cup unsalted butter
½ cup fresh mushrooms, chopped
½ cup ham, minced
½ cup green onions, finely minced
½ cup onions, minced
3 cloves garlic, minced
1 tbsp. soy flour
1 tbsp. all purpose flour

1 tsp. salt
1 tsp. white pepper
½ tsp. cayenne pepper
1 tsp. Tabasco® Sauce
¾ cup Beef Stock (see p. 86 for recipe)
   or beef broth
½ cup of rich red dry wine

Melt the butter in a medium saucepan over medium heat. Lightly sauté the mushrooms, ham, green onions, onions, and garlic for 5 minutes, stirring constantly. Add the flour and soy flour and cook for 5 more minutes, stirring constantly. Add the salt, white pepper, and Tabasco® Sauce and blend in well. Slowly add the stock to the pan and, using the wire whisk, blend it into the roux mixture. Add the wine and stir it into the sauce. Cook for 15 minutes over medium heat, stirring constantly. Remove from the heat. Makes about 2 cups of sauce.

Lagniappe: This is a wonderful sauce over beef, veal, chicken, or poached eggs. The sauce is named for the wine merchant, and when you taste it you'll know why. I try to use the same wine that I'll be serving at dinner to make this sauce to make sure it pairs well with the meal. You can make this sauce in advance and refrigerate it for later use. It will intensify in the refrigerator. To use, just heat over low heat until the sauce is hot and then serve.

Carbs per tablespoon: 8 g.
Net carbs per tablespoon: .6 g.
Calories per tablespoon: 42

CHEESE SAUCE

8 oz. Velveeta®, cut into large cubes
½ cup half-and-half cream
1 tsp. Tabasco® Sauce

In a medium saucepan over medium heat, add all the ingredients. Cook over low heat, stirring constantly until the sauce is smooth and all the cheese has melted. Pour warm over the vegetable or meat of your choice. Makes about 1½ cup of sauce. Serving size is 2 tbsp.

Lagniappe: It doesn't get any easier than this—a great cheese sauce with almost no effort. You can store any leftovers in the refrigerator until you are ready to use. Just heat and serve. Use this sauce over any vegetable that is enhanced by cheese. You can add a little variety by using other grated cheeses to the sauce.

Carbs per serving: 2.4 g.
Net Carbs per serving: 2.4 g.
Calories per serving: 77

SAUCE ESPAGNOLE

2 tbsp. pan drippings from cooked meat
1 tbsp. unsalted butter
1 cup onions, finely chopped
¼ cup carrots, finely minced
2 tbsp. celery, minced
¼ tbsp. bell pepper, minced
1 tbsp. all purpose flour
2 tbsp. soy flour
½ cup canned diced tomatoes
½ cup low sugar tomato sauce
½ cup Beef Stock (see p. 86) or beef
   broth

2 bay leaves
1 tsp. fresh ground black pepper
¼ tsp. thyme
½ tsp. oregano
1 tsp. fresh basil, minced
1 tsp. Tabasco® Sauce
1 tsp. garlic powder
1 tsp. Worcestershire sauce
1 tbsp. lemon juice
¼ cup fresh parsley, minced

In a medium skillet over medium heat, add the pan drippings and butter and let them get hot. Add the onions, carrots, celery, and bell pepper and sauté for 7 minutes or until limp, stirring constantly. Add the flour and soy flour and cook until the roux becomes light brown, stirring constantly. Add the tomatoes, tomato sauce, and Beef Stock and cook for 3 minutes or until the sauce begins to thicken. Season with the remaining ingredients. Serve warm over beef, pork, or chicken. Makes about 2 cups of sauce.

Lagniappe: This is a version of the classic French Sauce. It is a wonderful sauce on it's own over meats or poultry, but it can be used to enhance other sauces as well. You can make this in advance and refrigerate until you are ready to serve. Just reheat over low heat until the sauce is hot. Be sure to stir constantly.

Carbs per tablespoon: 1.5 g.
Net carbs per tablespoon: 1.1 g.
Calories per tablespoon: 18

SAUCE LYONNAISE

3 tbsp. butter
2 cups onions, finely chopped
½ cup dry white wine
½ cup white wine vinegar

1 recipe of Sauce Espagnole (see p. 32)
salt and fresh ground black pepper to taste

In a large saucepan over medium-high heat, add the butter and let it melt. When the butter is melted, add the onions and cook until they are very soft and almost dissolved, about 15 minutes. Add the wine and vinegar and cook until the liquid is reduced by half. Add the Sauce Espagnole and bring the sauce to a boil, then reduce the heat to simmer and cook for 5 minutes, stirring constantly. Season the sauce to taste with the salt and black pepper. Strain the sauce through a fine sieve and serve hot. Makes about 3 cups of sauce.

Lagniappe: This is the perfect sauce for roasted meats. Even though it is a version of Sauce Espagnole, it tastes do dramatically different that you wouldn't know if you hadn't made the sauce. The straining of the sauce gives it a different texture and leaves you with exceptional taste.

Carbs per tablespoon: 1.6 g.
Net carbs per tablespoon: 1.2 g.
Calories per tablespoon: 24

SAUCE ROUGE

1 stick unsalted butter
2 large red bell peppers
3 cloves garlic, minced
1 shallot, minced
2 tbsp. celery, minced
½ cup of Chenin Blanc white wine

¼ cup of white wine vinegar
1 tsp. Tabasco® Sauce
1 tsp. Seafood Seasoning Mix (see
  p. 17)
1 cup heavy whipping cream

In a medium saucepan over medium heat, add the butter and let it melt and get hot. Add the bell pepper, garlic, shallots, and celery. Sauté for 5 minutes, stirring often; remove from the heat and let cool. Add to a food processor with the wine, white wine vinegar, Tabasco® Sauce, and seasoning mix. Blend until the mixture is well blended and smooth. Add the whipping cream and blend together for 1 minute. Return to the saucepan and heat the sauce over low heat until it is warm throughout. Serve immediately. Makes about 2 cups of sauce.

Lagniappe: This is wonderful sauce for seafood. It makes a great sauce for lump crabmeat. I also use this sauce to make Shrimp Bisque. To make, just add 2 pounds of medium, uncooked, peeled, and deveined shrimp to the sauce with 1 more cup of heavy whipping cream and one more teaspoon of Seafood Seasoning Mix. Heat over low heat for 25 minutes, then serve hot. Serves 6 to 8.

Carbs per ⅛-cup serving: 2.3 g.
Net Carbs per ⅛-cup serving: 1.9
Calories per ⅛-cup serving: 216.4

For Shrimp Bisque:
Carbs per serving of 6 or 8: 7.2 g. or 5.4 g.
Net Carbs per serving of 6 or 8: 6.1 g. or 4.6 g.
Calories per serving of 6 or 8: 577 or 433

GRILLED STEAK MARINADE

3 cloves garlic, finely minced

2 tbsp. shallots, finely minced

½ cup soy sauce

⅓ cup dry red wine

2 tbsp. Splenda® sweetener

2 tsp. fresh ginger, finely minced

1 tbsp. fresh basil, crushed then finely chopped

1 tsp. fresh rosemary, finely chopped

¼ cup of green onions, finely minced

Put all the ingredients into a large glass bowl and stir until they are blended together well. Use as a marinade on your choice of steak. Excellent!

Lagniappe: This is a great way to make your steaks quite special. You will have your guest wondering what you've done to create such interesting steaks. You can use the same marinade for pork as well. I use dry white wine when I marinate chicken or shrimp, but I keep all the other ingredients the same. Be sure to use plenty of marinade as a basting sauce while you are grilling to enhance the flavor even more.

Carbs per basting: 1 g.
Net Carbs per basting: 1 g.
Calories per basting: 15

SAUCE "J.B."

½ cup no sugar added catsup (or low-carb catsup)

3 tbsp. horseradish

1 tbsp. balsamic vinegar

1 tsp. salt

1 tsp. fresh ground black pepper

1 tsp. Tabasco® Sauce

1 tsp. lemon juice

2 tsp. Creole mustard

1 tsp. Worcestershire sauce

Mix all the ingredients together, beating with a wire whisk until they are blended well. Chill in the refrigerator until you are ready to use. Use with beef dishes or with cooked seafood. Serve chilled. Makes about ¾ cup of sauce.

Lagniappe: This is an excellent sauce for any red meat or with a variety of seafood. It stores well in the refrigerator for up to one week. See note about balsamic vinegar on page 53.

Carbs per tablespoon: 2.3 g.
Net Carbs per tablespoon: 2 g.
Calories per tablespoon: 16.6

TARTAR SAUCE

2 cups mayonnaise
¼ cup sweet pickle relish
¼ cup onion, finely chopped
⅛ cup celery, finely chopped

2 tbsp. parsley, finely minced
1 tbsp. fresh lemon juice
1 tsp. Tabasco® Sauce
1 tsp. cream of tartar

Mix all the ingredients together in a medium mixing bowl with a wire whisk until well blended. Refrigerate for at least 2 hours before serving. Makes about 3 cups of sauce.

Lagniappe: Wonderful sauce for seafood. Can be stored in a bowl that his been tightly-covered jar for up to one year. It makes and excellent dipping sauce for any cooked seafood.

Carbs per tablespoon: .6 g.
Net Carbs per tablespoon: .5 g.
Calories per tablespoon: 21

REMOULADE SAUCE I

½ cup celery, finely chopped
½ cup green onions, finely chopped
½ cup hot mustard
½ cup extra virgin olive oil
¼ cup prepared horseradish
¼ cup Worcestershire sauce
½ cup low-carb catsup (sugar-free)

1 tsp. Tabasco® Sauce
1 tsp. fresh ground black pepper
½ cup red wine vinegar
1 packet of Splenda® sweetener
1 tsp. salt
1 tbsp. Paprika

In a large mixing bowl, combine all the ingredients until thoroughly mixed. Pour into a large container that has a tight lid and refrigerate for at least 4 hours to allow the flavors to blend. Serve chilled over peeled, boiled shrimp, crabmeat or crawfish. Makes about 3½ cups of Remoulade sauce. Serving size is ¼ cup.

Lagniappe: Keep this sauce chilled until you are ready to serve. It keeps well in the refrigerator for up to 6 days. You can use what you need and refrigerate the rest for later use. This sauce is great with any boiled seafood.

Carbs per serving: 5 g.
Net carbs per serving: 2.5 g.
Calories per serving: 87

REMOULADE SAUCE II

1 cup green onions, finely chopped
¼ cup celery, minced
3 cloves garlic, minced
¼ cup parsley, minced
¼ cup Creole mustard
2 tbsp. fresh lemon juice

2 tbsp. paprika
¼ cup white wine vinegar
1 tsp. salt
1 tsp. Tabasco® Sauce
1 tsp. black pepper
½ cup extra virgin olive oil

In a food processor, add all the ingredients except for the olive oil. Turn the processor on and blend at high speed until well mixed. Gradually drizzle in the olive through the top of the processor until it is all blended in well. Put in a container with a lid and refrigerate for 3 hours for the flavors to blend. Serve over boiled seafood of your choice. Makes about 2 cups of sauce. Serves 10.

Lagniappe: This is another version of remoulade sauce. It is one of the best remoulades made. You can make it two or three days before you need it and refrigerate until you are ready to serve. This remoulade has quite a different taste than the Remoulade I. Try them both to see which one is your favorite sauce.

Carbs per serving: 2.4 g.
Net carbs per serving: 1.7 g.
Calories per serving: 87

COCKTAIL SAUCE

1 cup low-carb catsup
¼ cup horseradish
1 tbsp. Worcestershire sauce
1 tbsp. lemon

1 tsp. Tabasco® Sauce
2 tsp. Equal® sweetener
½ tsp. salt

In a mixing bowl, add all the ingredients and stir together well until all the ingredients are blended. Store in the refrigerator until ready to use. Use this sauce for any boiled or broiled seafood. Makes about 1¼ cup of sauce.

Lagniappe: This is a great dipping sauce for any seafood. It keeps well in the refrigerator. You can find low-carb catsup in the low-carb section of your supermarket. There are a number of good varieties. Check them out to find out the one you like best. Adding the Equal® to it makes it closer to normal catsup sweetness.

Carbs per tbsp.: 2.0 g.
Net carbs per tbsp.: 1.9 g.
Calories per tbsp.: 17.6

LOW-CARB HOMEMADE CATSUP

15 small ripe tomatoes, skin removed
2 tsp. salt
2 tsp. fresh ground black pepper
1 tbsp. ground hot mustard
½ tsp. cloves
1 cup onions, chopped
1 cup red bell pepper, finely minced

2 cloves garlic, minced
2 cups white vinegar, distilled
2 tbsp. lemon juice, fresh
1 tbsp. Tabasco® Sauce
2 tbsp. celery, minced
3 tbsp. Splendä sweetener

Combine all the ingredients into a large pot and simmer over medium heat for 4 hours, covered. When it has cooked, remove from the heat and let cool. Strain it through a sieve. Bottle the catsup in pint jars and keep them tightly covered and stored in the refrigerator. Makes about 4 cups or 2 pints of catsup.

Lagniappe: While this does take time, if you are serious about excellent low-carb food with outstanding taste, this is the way to go. You can use the low-carb, store-bought catsup, which is good, but it is no comparison to homemade. This catsup will keep refrigerated and covered for up to 1 month. The difference is really in the net carbs. While low-carb, store-bought catsup has only 2 grams of carbs per tablespoon for both net carbs and carbs, this has only 1.2 g. of net carbs per tablespoon. If you use 1 cup, the difference is apparent. This homemade version has only 19 net carbs per cup and the store-bought version has 32. The taste is also a big added bonus!

Carbs per tablespoon: 1.5 g.
Net carbs per tablespoon: 1.2 g.
Calories per tablespoon: 9

LOW-CARB BARBECUE SAUCE

½ cup onions, minced
2 cloves garlic, finely minced
¼ cup vegetable oil
1 8-oz. can tomato sauce
1 cup low-carb catsup
¼ cup red wine vinegar

2 tbsp. Splenda® sweetener
2 tbsp. Worcestershire sauce
2 tbsp. mustard
1 tsp. salt
1 tsp. Tabasco® Sauce
2 tbsp. fresh parsley, finely minced

In a medium saucepan over medium heat, add the vegetable oil and let it get hot. Sauté the onions and garlic for 5 minutes, stirring often. Add the remaining ingredients and continue to cook for 15 minutes, stirring occasionally. This can be used like any other barbecue sauce. Makes about 2½ cups of sauce.

Lagniappe: This is a wonderful basting sauce for chicken, pork, beef, or fish. It can be refrigerated for up to 2 weeks. In fact, if you refrigerate it at least for 24 hours, it tends to be more flavorful. The flavors have a chance to enhance the entire sauce.

Carbs per tbsp.: 1.5 g.
Net Carbs per tbsp: 1.4 g.
Calories per tbsp: 23.4

HORSERADISH SAUCE FOR BEEF

2 cups of sour cream
1 cup of prepared horseradish
2 tsp. Tabasco® Sauce
¼ cup pecans, chopped

1 tsp. lime juice, fresh
1 tsp. salt
1 tsp. fresh ground black pepper
½ tsp. fresh basil, finely minced

In a large mixing bowl, mix together all the ingredients until they are thoroughly blended. Cover and chill for 1 hour to let the flavors blend. Serve chilled with roast beef. Makes about 3 cups of sauce.

Lagniappe: This is a wonderful sauce to serve with roast beef or grilled steaks. It keeps well and is full of flavor that enhances the taste of beef. You can make it in advance and refrigerate for up to 1 week.

Carbs per tablespoon of sauce: 1.8 g.
Net carbs per tablespoon of sauce: .8 g.
Calories per tablespoon: 27

RASPBERRY SAUCE

2 cups fresh raspberries, cleaned and rinsed
2 cloves garlic, minced
2 shallots, minced
2 tbsp. celery, minced
2 tbsp. red bell pepper, minced

1 stick unsalted butter
1 tbsp. balsamic vinegar
2 tsp. Tabasco® Sauce
1 tsp. Seafood Seasoning Mix (see p. 17)
½ cup heavy whipping cream

In a medium saucepan over medium heat add the butter and let it melt and get hot. Add 1 cup of the raspberries (reserving the remainder for later use), garlic, shallots, and celery. Sauté for 5 minutes, stirring often. Remove from the heat and let cool. Add to a food processor with the vinegar, Tabasco® Sauce, and seasoning mix. Blend until the mixture is well blended and smooth. Add the whipping cream and blend together for 1 minute. Return to the saucepan and add the reserved cup of raspberries and heat the sauce over low heat until it is warm throughout. Serve hot or cold. Makes about 2 cups of sauce.

Lagniappe: This is a wonderful sauce for seafood, pork, or poultry. It makes a great sauce for fish or on top of grilled pork chops. This sauce is good either hot or cold. It stores in the refrigerator for up to 4 days and freezes fairly well. It loses a little bit of potency, but is still quite good. See note about balsamic vinegar on page 53.

Carbs per ⅛-cup serving: 2.8 g.
Net Carbs per ⅛-cup serving: 1.7 g.
Calories per ⅛-cup serving: 139

WHISKEY SAUCE FOR BREAD PUDDING

1 tbsp. brown sugar
1¼ cup Splenda®
1 tsp. water
½ stick unsalted butter

1 egg, slightly beaten
2 egg yolks, slightly beaten
½ cup whiskey

In a medium saucepan over medium-high heat, add the brown sugar and let it cook, stirring constantly until it caramelizes and becomes a rich, dark brown. Remove from the heat and add the Splenda® and water. Set aside for later use. Melt the butter in another saucepan and, when melted, let it cool, but not solidify. Add the egg and yolks to the butter and whip with a wire whisk until the egg and butter are well mixed. Add the whiskey and the butter-egg mixture to the pan of Splenda® and return to medium-low heat. Using a wire whisk, stir the mixture until it begins to thicken; take care not to raise the temperature too high, which would cause the eggs to scramble. Serve over hot bread pudding or other desserts of your choice. Serves 10.

Lagniappe: This is a great treat for bread pudding or any cake. It adds a lot of flavor and makes the dish special. You can make this in advance and refrigerate until you are ready to use, just heat it over low heat, stirring constantly until the sauce is warm. You can make Rum Sauce by substituting dark rum for the whiskey and following the recipe as above. You can also make Bourbon Sauce by using bourbon instead of whiskey. The other famous sauce you can make is Brandy Sauce by substituting brandy for the whiskey in the recipe above. Anyway you make it, it's going to be good.

Note: This recipe calls for more Splenda® than Atkins® advises. However, the carb counts are still accurate.

Carbs per serving: 4.6 g.
Net carbs per serving: 4.6 g.
Calories per serving: 145

CHOCOLATE SAUCE

4 squares unsweetened chocolate
¼ cup heavy whipping cream
¼ cup half-and-half

½ cup Splenda® sweetener
½ tsp. vanilla extract

Put all ingredients in the top of a double boiler and cook over medium-high heat until the sauce is thick. The sauce should be thick but able to be poured. Serve warm. Serves 6.

Lagniappe: This is a good chocolate sauce to serve over low-carb ice cream, pies, or cakes. You can store for up to 1 week in the refrigerator for later use. Just heat over low heat until the sauce is warm and ready to serve. This gives you the thick, chocolate taste and texture of a great chocolate sauce. But it is still low-carb!

Carbs per serving: 8 g.
Net carbs per serving: 4.0 g.
Calories per serving: 272

Appetizers

SHRIMP NEW IBERIA

2 tbsp. extra virgin olive oil
1 tbsp. shallots, minced
3 cloves garlic, minced
2 pounds shrimp, peeled and deveined
1 large red bell pepper, cut into strips
1 large yellow bell pepper, cut into strips
1 large onion, sliced lengthwise
1 cup celery, cut into strips

1 cup carrots, cut into strips about 3 inches long
3 medium jalapeno, cut into thin circles
1 tbsp. Splenda® sweetener
2 tbsp. fresh basil, minced
2 tsp. Seafood Seasoning Mix (see p. 17)
3 whole bay leaves
½ tsp. thyme, dried
½ cup fresh parsley, finely minced

In a large, heavy skillet over medium-high heat, heat the olive oil until it begins to pop. Add the shallots and garlic and sauté for 4 minutes. Add half of the shrimp and sauté until they turn a solid white color, about 5 minutes. Repeat the process for the other half of the shrimp. Place the shrimp in a large, glass bowl that has a lid. Mix together the bell peppers, onion, celery, carrots, jalapeno, sweetener, basil, Seafood Seasoning Mix, bay leaves, and thyme in a medium-sized pot. Pour the cup of vinegar on top of the vegetables and bring the mixture to a boil, then reduce the heat to simmer and cover. Cook for about 5 minutes or until tender. When the mixture is done, pour over the shrimp and stir together well. Tightly cover the shrimp and refrigerate for at least 6 hours, but it is better if it's 24 to 36 hours. Serve chilled right from the refrigerator. Serve with plenty of the pickled vegetables. Serves 10.

Lagniappe: This is a wonderful appetizer to bring to potluck dinners. You can make this up to 3 days in advance. Store it tightly in the refrigerator. You can also use this recipe to make Crab Fingers New Iberia. Just use cracked crab claw fingers in the place of the shrimp. You do not have to sauté the crab fingers at all; just skip over that step and proceed with the rest of the recipe. Be sure to store both the shrimp and the crab fingers in a tightly covered bowl or jar while in the refrigerator. This is a great party food!

Carbs per serving: 6.5 g.
Net carbs per serving: 4.7 g.
Calories per serving: 137

CREAMY CRAB DISH IOTA

2 8-oz. packages cream cheese, cut into blocks
½ pound Brie cheese
½ cup green onions, chopped

1 tsp. Seafood Seasoning Mix (see p. 17)
1 pound lump crabmeat
½ cup spicy salsa
¼ cup parsley, minced

In a medium saucepan over medium-low heat, melt the cream cheese and Brie until creamy, stirring constantly. Remove from the heat and add the remaining ingredients and blend together well. Serve either hot or cold with fresh vegetables or low-carb tortillas. Serves 10.

Lagniappe: This is a good dish either hot or cold. If you serve it cold, use it as you would any cheese spread. If you serve it hot, you can use it as a dip. Cucumbers, squash, bell peppers, celery, and turnips are excellent choices of vegetables.

Carbs per serving: 2.9 g.
Net carbs per serving: 2.55 g.
Calories per serving: 244

CRAB DIP BELLE AMIEE

2 packages (8 oz. ea.) cream cheese
1 cup plain yogurt (whole milk)
2 tbsp. mustard, Dijon
1 tsp. Tabasco® Sauce
1 tbsp. fresh lemon juice
1 tsp. fresh basil, minced
1 tsp. Seafood Seasoning Mix (see p.xx)

1 tbsp. Worcestershire sauce
1 pound lump crabmeat
½ cup red bell pepper, finely diced
¼ cup green bell pepper, finely diced
½ cup green onion bottoms, minced
¼ cup of fresh parsley, minced

In a medium saucepan over medium heat, add the first eight ingredients, stirring constantly. When the cream cheese is melted, add the remaining ingredients and blend together until it is well blended. Serve warm as a dip. Serves 10.

Lagniappe: Crabmeat makes any dish delightful. This is a quick and easy recipe and will thrill your guests. Don't let the ease fool you; it might be simple but the flavors blend together well. This doesn't have to be used only as a dip. Put it into the center of a low-carb tortilla and roll it up like a crepe. Serve warm as a wonderful roll-up. Use vegetables cut into pieces for dipping. You can also use very low-carb toasted bread triangles. It's easy and delicious.

Carbs per serving: 4.2 g.
Net carbs per serving: 3.8 g.
Calories per serving: 183

QUICK CRAB DIP

1 cup cheddar cheese, shredded
½ cup MontereyJack cheese, shredded
1 8-oz. package cream cheese
½ cup half-and-half

1 tsp. Tabasco® Sauce
1 tbsp. Worcestershire sauce
1 tsp. onion powder
½ cup low-carb beer

Combine all the ingredients in the top of a double boiler and bring to a boil. Stir the cheese mixture until it is completely melted. Add the crabmeat and gently stir it in. Cook for 2 minutes, then pour into a chaffing dish and serve. Serve 15. Use vegetables or low-carb chips to dip.

Lagniappe: This is quick and easy and it'll bring raves. It can be made up to 3 days in advance. Refrigerate until ready to serve. Just reheat over low heat until melted.

Carbs per serving: 1.2 g.
Net carbs per serving: 1.2 g.
Calories per serving: 110

LUMP CRABMEAT COCKTAIL

1 tbsp. Worcestershire sauce
2 tbsp. lemon juice
1 tbsp. lime juice
1 tbsp. catsup (low-carb)
1 cup mayonnaise
1 tsp. Creole mustard
1 tbsp. balsamic vinegar
½ cup celery, minced
3 cloves garlic, minced
¼ cup green onion bottoms, finely chopped
2 tsp. Tabasco® Sauce
1 tsp. salt
1½ tsp. fresh ground black pepper
1 tsp. fresh basil minced
1 tsp. paprika
1 lb. lump crabmeat

Mix together all the ingredients except the crabmeat in a medium-sized mixing bowl with a wire whisk. When well blended, gently add the crabmeat to the mixture and fold it in. Cover the bowl tightly and refrigerate for 3 hours. To serve, place in cocktail serving glasses or a cocktail dish. Serve chilled. Serves 6.

Lagniappe: This is wonderful eating! There is almost nothing better than lump crabmeat, which this appetizer basically is. The only problem I ever have with this recipe is keeping the plastic wrap on until I am ready to serve! That's because everyone in the house is constantly testing to make sure it's doing okay. Keep it hidden if you want to be sure you'll have enough for your guests.

Carbs per serving: 2.9 g.
Net carbs per serving: 2.2 g.
Calories per serving: 356

Note: I am using balsamic vinegar for its intense flavor. It does not meet the Atkins® guidelines. If you want to, you can use red wine vinegar as a substitute.

SHRIMP YOLANDE

20 pre-cooked and peeled shrimp with tails (about 20 count per lb.)
10 large jalapenos, cut in half
20 slices of thin cut smoked bacon

1 lb. block of Monterey Jack cheese, cut into 20 pieces about the size of the shrimp

Preheat the oven to 425 degrees. Butterfly the shrimp and place half of a jalapeno and a piece of cheese between each shrimp tail. Wrap the shrimp from the top to the tail with the bacon. Be sure to cover all the shrimp except for the tail. Place on a non-stick baking pan and bake until the bacon is cooked, about 15 minutes. Remove and place on a serving platter. Serve hot. Serves 10 as an appetizer or 5 as a main dish.

Lagniappe: You can cook this in the oven, and it also cooks very well on a George Forman® grill. I've pan-fried it with great success as well. It even cooks nicely on the barbecue pit; just make sure to put a piece of foil under the shrimp to keep them from falling through. There is nothing worse than a bacon-wrapped shrimp in the coals! You can make this in advance and refrigerate to serve later. Just pop it in the oven for 5 minutes at 300 degrees before serving. I like to cook a few extra and freeze them in an air-tight, plastic sandwich bag, so if I have unexpected company, I have a quick treat. You can thaw them in the microwave on 30 percent power until thawed and then heat them at 100 percent for 1 minute then serve. This is delightful eating. It's this dish that started my sister, Yolande on the low-carb trail. She said, "If I can eat this and really lose weight, I can do it!" She did and she has.

Carbs per appetizer serving: 1.7g.
Net carbs per appetizer serving: 1.5 g.
Calories per appetizer serving: 238

Carbs per main dish serving: 3.4 g.
Net carbs per main dish serving: 3.1 g.
Calories per main dish serving: 476

FRESH OYSTER COCKTAIL

24 fresh whole raw oysters
¼ tbsp. low-carb catsup (sugar-free)
¼ Worcestershire sauce
2 tsp. Tabasco® Sauce
¼ cup fresh lemon juice

3 tbsp. horseradish
2 tsp. salt
2 tsp. fresh ground black pepper
¼ cup celery, minced
3 cloves garlic, finely minced

Dry each of the oysters on paper towels. Divide the oysters into 4 cocktail glasses or serving dishes, each with 6 oysters. Mix together all the remaining ingredients in a mixing bowl until well blended. Pour over each of the glasses of oysters and slightly stir. Cover with plastic wrap and refrigerate for 2 hours. Serve chilled. Serves 4.

Lagniappe: The perfect raw oyster cocktail. You will find it easy but full of flavor. You can make up it to 48 hours in advance and refrigerate until you are ready to serve. This is wonderful party food. Decorate the glass with a slice of lemon and a heart of celery stick. Excellent!

Carbs per serving: 9.9 g.
Net carbs per serving: 9.2 g.
Calories per serving: 117

OYSTER CHERRIES

20 large cherry tomatoes
1 8-oz. package cream cheese, softened
1 green onion, chopped
1 clove garlic, minced
½ cup Swiss cheese, shredded
1 tsp. Tabasco® Sauce
1 tsp. fresh ground black pepper
½ tsp. onion powder
1 tsp. fresh basil, finely minced
1 oz. cognac
1 7.5-oz. container smoked oysters
1 tsp. fresh lemon juice
¼ cup fresh parsley, minced
4 oz. heavy whipping cream, whipped stiff

Rinse the tomatoes, pick the stem, and cut off the tops. Take out the insides with a melon scoop and turn them upside down on paper towels to drain. Place the tomato centers in a small skillet and heat over high heat until they are reduced to about 2 tbsp. sauce. Place the tomato sauce in a food processor with all the ingredients except for the oysters, lemon juice, parsley, and whipping cream; blend at high speed until the mixture is creamy and smooth. Chop the oysters in half and place them in the processor and blend using pulse for 10 seconds. Refrigerate for 2 hours. When the mixture has set, gently fold in the lemon juice, parsley, and whipping cream into the cream cheese mixture. Stuff the mixture into each of the 20 cherry tomatoes. Chill until ready to serve. Serves 10.

Lagniappe: This is a pretty buffet table dish. The bright red of the cherry tomatoes makes any buffet look nice. It is also a great dish to bring to a covered dish. You won't have to worry that someone else brought the same thing. It is also a wonderful side dish to set off any plate you serve. It takes a little time to stuff the tomatoes, but it isn't difficult.

Carbs per serving: 4 g.
Net carbs per serving: 2.4 g.
Calories per serving: 169

BAKED OYSTERS BOURBON

2 slices low-carb bread, (5 carbs per slice)
butter-flavored vegetable oil spray
2 tbsp. unsalted butter
2 tbsp. extra virgin olive oil
1 medium onion, finely chopped
2 cloves garlic, finely minced
¼ cup of celery, minced
2 tsp. Italian seasoning

¼ cup of Romano cheese, grated
¼ cup of Parmesan cheese, grated
1 tsp. fresh ground black pepper
1 tsp. salt
1 tsp. cayenne pepper
1 tbsp. fresh lemon juice
1 qt. fresh oysters, drained as much as possible

Take the two slices of low-carb bread and spray them generously with the butter-flavored, vegetable oil spray. Bake in an oven preheated to 225 degrees until the bread has dried out completely. When the bread has dried, put it into a food processor and blend until it becomes breadcrumbs. Set aside for later use. In a large saucepan over medium heat, melt the butter and olive oil. Sauté the onions, garlic, and celery until tender (about 3 minutes), stirring constantly. Remove from the heat, add all the remaining ingredients, and mix together well. Pour into a large baking dish (8 x 10 or 12 inches) and bake at 425 for 20 minutes or until the oysters begin to plump up and the ends curl. Serve hot. Serves 8 as an appetizer or main dish.

Lagniappe: You can pour the oysters into individual baking dishes for a nice touch, or you can spoon the oysters onto individual plates when you are ready to serve. Oysters are excellent baked and taste quite different from the raw ones you might have eaten. A baked oyster has a unique, tantalizing taste. As an alternative, you can put the oysters on individual half shells and serve as individual items.

Carbs per serving: 6.2 g.
Net Carbs per serving: 5.5 g.
Calories per serving: 174

PICKLED MUSHROOMS

½ cup dark rum
½ cup fresh lemon juice
2 tbsp. white distilled vinegar
¼ cup red bell pepper, diced
2 tbsp. celery, minced
3 cloves garlic, crushed then minced
2 tbsp. shallots, finely minced
1 tsp. salt

1 tsp. fresh coarsely ground black
  pepper
1 tsp. fresh oregano, minced
2 bay leaves
2 tsp. fresh basil, minced
1 tsp. fresh rosemary, crushed
1 pound fresh mushrooms, cleaned of
  grit

Mix together all the ingredients in a large, glass mixing bowl and blend well. Cover tightly with plastic wrap and refrigerate for at least 12 hours. Serve chilled. Serves 6.

Lagniappe: These mushrooms can be stored for up to one week in the refrigerator. This is an excellent party food and a great appetizer. It can also be used as a vegetable side dish. You can change the rum to any other flavor of alcohol you like, although dark rum lends itself well to this dish.

Carbs per serving: 5.2 g.
Net Carbs per serving: 4.3 g.
Calories per serving: 76

CUCUMBER SANDWICHES

1 8-oz. package cream cheese, softened
¼ tsp. Seafood Seasoning Mix (see p. 17)
2 tbsp. green onions, finely minced
1 clove garlic, finely minced
3 tbsp. red bell pepper, finely diced
2 medium cucumbers
1 tsp. fresh parsley, minced

In a medium mixing bowl, add the cream cheese, seasoning mix green onions, garlic, and red bell pepper. Blend together or mix with an electric mixer until well blended. Set aside and let stand. Wash and clean the cucumbers, then slice them into circles that are ¼-inch thick. Spread a generous amount of the cream cheese mixture on each cucumber slice. Sprinkle a little bit of parsley on each slice of cucumber. Serve chilled. Serves 12.

Lagniappe: This looks simple and it is! But the taste is delicious. It's a good appetizer or party treat. You can even make them in advance. This is a tasty, low-carb snack to keep stored in the fridge for quick treats any time of the day.

Carbs per serving of 10: 1.6 g.
Net Carbs per serving: 1.3 g.
Calories per serving: 85.2

Carbs per serving of 12: 1.3 g.
Net Carbs per serving: 1.1 g.
Calories per serving: 71

SPICY HAM BALLS

2 cups ham, finely chopped
2 8-oz. packages cream cheese,
   softened
½ cup pickapeppa sauce

2 tsp. Tabasco® Sauce
3 tbsp. onions, finely minced
2 cups pecans, finely chopped
paprika to dust balls

In a large mixing bowl, add all the ingredients except the paprika and blend together until smooth; cover the bowl and refrigerate for 5 hours or until the mixture is somewhat firm. Line a large tray with wax paper. Using a tablespoon, scoop out about 2 tablespoons of mixture and roll it into a ball with your hand. Place on the wax paper and repeat the process until all the mixture is used. It should make about 30 ham balls. Dust the balls lightly with the paprika and cover the tray with plastic wrap and refrigerate. When you are ready to serve, arrange the ham balls on a nice serving tray. Serve chilled. Serves 10 to 12.

Lagniappe: This is a good way to use leftover ham. Be sure to chop the ham finely or chop it in a food processor. You can also add a little shredded sharp cheddar cheese to the mix for a slightly different taste. I sometimes like to serve both balls, some with the cheese added and some without. It's like having two appetizers, since they taste so different. Either way, these ham balls will be a hit!

Carbs per serving of 12: 5.4 g.
Net Carbs per serving of 12: 4.3 g.
Calories per serving of 12: 284.5

Carbs per serving of 10: 6.5 g.
Net Carbs per serving of 10: 5.2 g.
Calories per serving of 10: 341

GUACAMOLE CAJUN

4 ripe avocados
1 large fresh tomato, peeled and diced
½ cup onions, minced
2 cloves garlic, minced
2 tbsp. red bell pepper, diced finely
2 tbsp. lime juice
1 tsp. salt

1 tsp. chili powder
¼ tsp. cumin
1 tsp. Tabasco® Sauce
½ tsp. fresh ground black pepper
2 tbsp. fresh parsley, minced
4 cups lettuce, shredded

Peel the avocado and place into a medium mixing bowl; mash until there are no lumps left. Mix together all the remaining ingredients, except for the lettuce, until well blended. Place the lettuce on top of each of six plates. Put an equal amount of guacamole on top of each plate of shredded lettuce and serve chilled. Serves 6.

Lagniappe: While this salad can be served right after making, it is better when you let the guacamole stand in the refrigerator for 2 hours before serving. It can actually be made and refrigerated up to 48 hours in advance. Store in a tightly-covered bowl and, just before serving, stir the guacamole a few times with a fork. There may be a slight darkening of the salad after standing for more than 24 hours, but the taste is not affected. By stirring it, the beautiful, light-green color is restored.

Carbs per serving: 9.1 g.
Net Carbs per serving: 6.1 g.
Calories per serving: 29

DEVILED EGGS

12 eggs, hard boiled
12 black olives, finely chopped
12 stuffed green olives, finely chopped
3 tbsp. celery, finely chopped

3 tbsp. red bell pepper, finely diced
¼ cup mayonnaise
1 tbsp. Dijon mustard

Cut the boiled eggs in half and remove the yolks to a medium-sized mixing bowl. Add the remaining ingredients and mash together. Fill the egg white halves with the mixture and dust with paprika. Serve immediately or serve chilled from the refrigerator. Serves 6.

Lagniappe: This is a low-carb version of deviled eggs because it uses olives instead of the sweet pickle relish, which has a bit too many sugar carbs. You can use dill pickle relish in place of the olives if you like, but the olives are a nice touch and a great taste.

Carbs per serving: 2.8 g.
Net Carbs per serving: 1.8 g.
Calories per serving: 218

CAJUN SPINACH DIP

1 10-oz. package frozen spinach, thawed

1 8-oz. package cream cheese, softened

3 tbsp. half-and-half cream

8 oz. Velveeta® cheese, cut into cubes

1 medium onion, chopped

2 cloves garlic, minced

½ cup bell pepper, diced

1 medium tomato, chopped

½ cup jalapeno peppers, chopped

1 tsp. paprika

½ tsp. salt

½ tsp. black pepper

¼ cup fresh parsley, minced

Thoroughly drain all the water out of the spinach. You can wrap 6 paper towels around the spinach and press down hard until most of the water has been forced out. Place the cream cheese into a food processor and beat until it is smooth and creamy. Add all the remaining ingredients and blend until well mixed. Pour into a medium-sized saucepan and heat just until the dip starts to bubble. Turn the heat down to low and pour into a chaffing dish or a dish that will keep the dip warm. Serve with fresh vegetables or with a low-carb tortilla chips. Serve warm. Serves 12 as a dip.

Lagniappe: This is a great party food. Spinach dip is always a hit. This low-carb version will be sure to please even the picky eater. You can make this dip in advance and store in the refrigerator for up to 5 days before serving. Just heat on the stove until warm or in the microwave.

Carbs per serving: 6.8 g.
Net Carbs per serving: 5.1 g.
Calories per serving: 97

SPICY PECANS

4 cups whole pecan halves
¼ cup salt
¼ cup Tabasco® Sauce

1 tbsp. fresh basil, minced
4 cups water
1 tsp. cayenne pepper

In a medium-sized mixing bowl add all the ingredients except for the cayenne pepper. Stir until the salt is dissolved. Let the pecans sit in the seasoned water for 3 hours. Drain the pecans in a colander and let them sit in the colander for 2 hours. Preheat the oven to 300 degrees. Spread the pecans out flat on a large cookie sheet. Sprinkle evenly with the cayenne pepper and bake for 25 minutes, then stir them well and bake for 25 more minutes. Remove from the oven and let them cool for 20 minutes. Serve as an appetizer. Serves 20.

Lagniappe: This is a make-ahead dish. You can make the pecans up to one week before you need them. Just store in a dry container with a tight lid. Keeping them stored helps intensify the flavors. If you like, you can heat them for just a few minutes before serving. Hot pecans really taste better that those served at room temperature, but either way they are good.

Carbs per serving: 3 g.
Net Carbs per serving: 1 g.
Calories per serving: 149

CAJUN EGGPLANT DIP

2 small eggplants (about 14 oz. each)
2 tbsp. extra virgin olive oil
1 large onion, chopped
2 cloves garlic, minced
¼ cup celery, chopped
¼ cup bell pepper, chopped

1 medium cayenne pepper, finely minced
2 tbsp. lemon juice
1 tbsp. balsamic vinegar
1½ tsp. salt
2 tsp. fresh ground black pepper

Preheat the oven to 425 degrees. Peel the eggplant and slice it into 5 pieces each. On a non-stick baking dish that has been sprayed with cooking oil, place the eggplant slices so that they don't touch each other. Bake for 35 minutes, uncovered. While the eggplant is baking, in a heavy, medium skillet over medium-high heat, add the olive oil and let it get hot. Add the onion, garlic, celery, bell pepper, and cayenne pepper. Sauté for 7 minutes, stirring often. When the eggplant has baked for 35 minutes, add it to a food processor with all the other ingredients, including the sautéed vegetables. Blend at high speed until it is smooth. Serve with low-carb tortillas, pita bread, or Atkins® low-carb bread. Serve hot or cold. Makes about 3 ½ cups of dip. Serves 10.

Lagniappe: This is the dip for eggplant lovers, but it'll surprise you how many people will eat this dip and ask what it is. You have to be the judge of whether to tell them or not. The eggplant is so often maligned and under-used. It is a great vegetable with lots of taste and a unique flavor. I like to use this dip as a spread on sandwiches to give them that delicious flavor.

Carbs per serving: 4.8 g.
Net Carbs per serving: 3.4 g.
Calories per serving: 44

GREEN ONION HAM ROLL-UPS

2 whole green onions, washed trimmed and cut into thirds
1 clove garlic, cut in half
2 tbsp. bell pepper
2 tbsp. celery, chopped
1 tsp. Seafood Seasoning Mix (see p. 17)
1 tsp. Tabasco® Sauce
1 tsp. Worcestershire sauce

1 package (8 oz.) cream cheese, softened
1 cup sharp cheddar cheese, shredded
½ cup Monterey Jack cheese, shredded
½ cup Swiss cheese, shredded
⅛ cup fresh parsley, minced
16 slices of deli-quality ham, sliced about 7/16-inch thick (about 1 lb.)

In a food processor add the green onions, garlic, bell pepper, and celery; blend at high speed until it is finely chopped. Add the seasoning mix, Tabasco®, Worcestershire, and cream cheese; mix on high speed until it is well mixed. Scrape the sides with a rubber spatula two or three times to be sure that all the cheese is blended. Add the cheddar, Monterey Jack, Swiss cheese, and parsley and blend until the cheeses are well mixed with the cream cheese. Remove the mixture from the processor and put into a plastic container with a tight top. Refrigerate while you prepare the ham. Cut the ham in half lengthwise and place about 2 tbsp. of cheese mixture into the center of each piece of ham. Roll the ham like a cigar and place them on a serving platter or on individual serving plates. Makes 32 ham rolls. Serves 8.

Lagniappe: You can make these rolls in advance and store them tightly-covered in the refrigerator for up to 6 days. I like to keep them stored in the refrigerator for instant, low-carb snacks. You can be creative about these rolls and keep multiple varieties stored for snacks, appetizers or for wonderful light lunches or brunches. See the index for the different varieties of ham rolls, turkey rolls, and roast beef rolls.

Carbs per serving: 2.8 g.
Net carbs per serving: 2.6 g.
Calories per serving: 436

GREEK HAM ROLL-UPS

2 clove garlic, cut in half
¼ cup Lindsay Olivada® spread
2 tbsp. green onions, minced
2 tbsp. red bell pepper
1 tbsp. celery, chopped
1 tsp. Seafood Seasoning Mix (see p. 17)
1 tsp. Tabasco® Sauce
1 tsp. lime juice
2 tsp. Worcestershire sauce

1 8-oz. package cream cheese, softened
1 cup Provolone cheese, shredded
½ cup sharp cheddar cheese, shredded
½ cup Gouda cheese, shredded
½ tsp. oregano
½ tsp. sweet basil
16 slices of deli-quality ham, sliced about ¹⁄₁₆-inch thick (about 1 lb.)

In a food processor add the garlic, Olivada® spread, green onions, bell pepper, and celery; blend at high speed until it is finely chopped. Add the seasoning mix, Tabasco®, lime juice, Worcestershire, and cream cheese; mix on high speed until it is well blended. Scrape the sides with a rubber spatula two or three times to be sure that all the cheese is blended. Add the shredded cheeses, oregano, and basil; blend until the cheeses are completely mixed with the cream cheese. Remove the mixture from the processor and put into plastic bowl that has a tight top. Refrigerate while you prepare the ham. Cut the ham in half lengthwise; remove the cheese mixture from the refrigerator and place about 2 tbsp. of cheese mixture onto the center of each piece of ham. Roll the ham like you would a cigar and place them on a serving platter or on individual serving plates. Makes 32 ham rolls. Serves 8.

Lagniappe: The olive spread makes these rolls completely different in both taste and texture. The addition of Gouda cheese truly makes these tasty treats worth trying. I really like to keep multiple varieties on hand to add to the "spice of life" variety. You have to keep your snack choices interesting and fun to stay on your new diet.

Carbs per serving: 2.6 g.
Net carbs per serving: 2.3 g.
Calories per serving: 296

ROASTED PEPPER TURKEY ROLL-UPS

¼ cup sweet roasted red pepper strips

2 tbsp zesty pepper rings, chopped

1 tbsp. green onions, minced

1 clove garlic, minced

1 tbsp. celery, minced

1 tsp. Seafood Seasoning Mix (see p. 17)

1 tsp. Tabasco® Sauce

1 tsp. fresh basil, minced

1 8-oz. package cream cheese, softened

1 cup Swiss cheese, grated

½ cup Mozzarella cheese

1 cup colby cheese, grated

1 tbsp fresh parsley, minced

1 lb. deli turkey, cut about ¹⁄₁₆-inch thick

Put the first 8 ingredients into a food processor and pulse 10 times, then add the cream cheese and blend until the mixture is smooth. Add the cheeses and the fresh parsley and blend until the cheeses are well mixed. Remove from the processor and place in a bowl. Set aside until you are ready to use. Cut the turkey slices each onto three strips each about 1½ inches wide. Spoon about 1 tbsp. of the mixture into the center of each of the strips of turkey and roll the turkey around the cheese mixture, like you would roll a crepe. Place each roll on a serving platter and repeat the process until all the turkey is used. Makes about 52 Turkey Roll-Ups.

Lagniappe: This is a wonderful spread to use on turkey, ham, or any deli meat you like to use. You can use ham and make Roasted Pepper Ham Roll-Ups or use pastrami and make Roasted Pepper Pastrami Roll-Ups. Or use the meat of your choice and make the roll-up of your dreams! I like to make a variety and serve a mixed platter of roll-ups as a feature of any buffet or brunch that I serve. Your imagination is your key!

Carbs per roll-up: trace
Net carbs per roll-up: trace
Calories per roll-up: 84

SPINACH AND HAM ROLL-UPS

1 8-oz. package cream cheese, softened

½ Spinach Salad Dressing recipe (see p. 123)

½ cup sharp cheddar cheese, grated

1 lb. deli ham, sliced about ⅟₁₆-inch thick, cut in half lengthwise

In a food processor with a metal blade, blend the cream cheese until smooth. Add the Spinach Dressing and cheddar cheese and blend until it is well blended. Remove from the processor to a bowl and spread about 2 tbsp. of the cheese mixture to the middle of each half-slice of ham and roll the ham up as you would a crepe. Repeat the process until all the cheese mixture and ham are used. Makes about 32 roll-ups.

Lagniappe: This is an excellent party or snack food. It's great in a buffet or as a light lunch meal with a salad or soup. I like to keep these roll-ups made in the refrigerator to use as snacks. If you're starving, it gives you a quick alternative to the high-carb foods that are screaming "Eat me!" This is a quick and tasty snack. Sometimes I just make the mixture and let it sit in the refrigerator. When I'm ready to eat, I just take the amount of ham I need and make the number of roll-ups I want.

Carbs per Roll-Up: 1.5 g.
Net Carbs per Roll-Up: 1.2 g.
Calories per Roll-Up: 51

GUACAMOLE CAJUN ROLL-UPS

1 8-oz. package cream cheese, softened
½ Guacamole Cajun recipe (see p. 61)
1 tsp. Tabasco® Sauce

1 cup Monterey cheese, grated
½ cup Edam cheese, grated
1 lb. deli ham, sliced about ⅟₁₆-inch thick, cut in half lengthwise

In a food processor with a metal blade, blend the cream cheese until smooth. Add the Guacamole Cajun, Tabasco® Sauce, and cheeses and blend until it is well blended. Remove from the processor to a bowl and spread about 2 tbsp. of the cheese mixture to the middle of each half slice of ham and roll the ham up as you would a crepe. Repeat the process until all the cheese mixture and ham are used. Makes about 32 roll-ups.

Lagniappe: Excellent party or snack food. Just use your imagination to make the roll-ups of your choice. I like to keep these roll-ups in the refrigerator to use as quick snacks to help you at those times when you are busy and need something to eat quickly. I keep a few different mixtures at a time in the fridge, so I have a choice when I'm hungry or ready to eat.

Carbs per Roll-Up: 1.1 g.
Net carbs per Roll-Up: .8 g.
Calories per Roll-Up: 74

LUMP CRABMEAT ROLL-UPS

½ cup mayonnaise
½ cup green onions, minced
1 cup Gouda cheese, shredded
½ cup Swiss cheese
¼ cup roasted red peppers, diced

1 tsp. Seafood Seasoning Mix (see p. 17)
½ tsp. fresh basil, minced
1 cup fresh lump crabmeat
6 low-carb (3 net carbs each) tortillas

In a medium-sized mixing bowl, combine all the ingredients except for the crabmeat and the tortillas. Fold the crab meat into the cheese mixture, taking care not to tear apart the large lump pieces. Place the mixture equally into the top part of each of the tortillas and gently roll the tortillas as you would a crepe or cigar. Place them seam down on a plate microwave on high power for 1 minute. It should melt the cheese and just get the roll-ups warm, not hot. Cut the tortillas into circles about ¾-inch thick. It should make about 6 circles for each tortilla. Serve warm or chilled. Makes 36 circles.

Lagniappe: This is another great roll-up to serve as a snack, brunch, lunch, or as a great appetizer. They keep well in the refrigerator for up to three days. This is a great snack that will kill hunger pains that strike at anytime. The nice thing about a low-carb diet is that when you are hungry . . . you eat! As long as it is low-carb!

Carbs per circle: 2.8 g.
Net carbs per circle: 1 g.
Calories per circle: 46

STUFFED JALAPENOS

1 8-oz. can mild jalapenos, seeded
ice water to cover
1 8-oz. package cream cheese
½ cup sharp cheddar cheese, grated
3 tbsp. onions, minced

3 tbsp. red bell pepper, finely diced
3 tbsp. sour cream
1 tsp. Tabasco® Sauce
2 tsp. Worcestershire sauce

Wash the jalapenos with cold water and cut them in half lengthwise. Place the cut jalapenos in a small bowl and cover with ice water, then set aside for later use. In another mixing bowl, cream the remaining items either in a food processor or with an electric mixer until smooth. Remove the jalapenos from the cold water and drain them on paper towels. Stuff each of the jalapeno halves with the cream cheese mixture, place on a serving platter and cover them tightly with plastic wrap, and refrigerate until you are ready to serve. Serve chilled. Serves 6.

Lagniappe: I use the mild jalapenos because there are so many people who can't take the heat of hot jalapenos. I personally like them better. Interestingly enough, the stuffing helps to cool your mouth right after the peppers make it hot. The cream cheese and sour cream have enzymes that have a cooling effect on the capsaicin oil that makes the pepper hot. It's sort of like taking a cold and hot shower all at once. (Isn't there a spa that does that for you and charges an arm and a leg for the service? Here you get it for the price of the stuffed peppers!) This can be exciting or to some perhaps a little idiotic! This is a simple recipe but delightfully delicious.

Carbs per serving: 4.7 g.
Net carbs per serving: 4.1 g.
Calories per serving: 266

CREAMY GREEN ONION DIP

½ cup mayonnaise

1 cup sour cream

¼ cup green onions, very finely minced

1 tsp. Tabasco® Sauce

1 clove garlic, very finely minced

1 tsp. Worcestershire sauce

1 tsp. salt

1 tbsp celery, very finely minced

½ tsp. onion powder

1 packet Equal® sweetener

In a medium mixing bowl, combine all ingredients and mix well. Cover tightly with plastic wrap and refrigerate for 2 hours. Serve chilled. Makes 1½ cup of dip.

Lagniappe: Serve with raw vegetables of your choice. This is a crowd pleaser. Everyone always has onion dip, but this one is a little different. You can make it up to 3 days in advance and store in the refrigerator, tightly covered. An excellent dip to take to a party.

Carbs per tbsp.: .64 g.
Net carbs per tbsp.: .6 g.
Calories per tbsp.: 55

CHOPPED CHICKEN LIVER DIP

1 lb. chicken livers
1 tsp. Chicken Seasoning Mix (see p. 18)
½ cup onions, chopped
2 cloves garlic, minced

2 tbsp. celery, minced
2 boiled eggs, peeled and sliced
1 tsp. Tabasco® Sauce
1 tsp. lemon juice
¼ cup mayonnaise

Preheat the oven to 400 degrees. Bake the chicken livers for 25 minutes or until they are brown and cooked through. Remove from the heat and let them cool. When cool, add the liver and the remaining ingredients to a food processor and blend full speed until all the liver is completely blended. Remove and put into a serving bowl, cover, and chill for 1 hour. Serve chilled. Serves 10.

Lagniappe: This is almost like a fine paté! But it is made so fast and easily. I like to serve this with celery sticks and cucumber slices, but it's almost so good you could eat it with a spoon. You can make it in advance and refrigerate for up to 48 hours. I don't like to serve liver after two days, but you are safe until then, as long as the dip is refrigerated. What a treat!

Carbs per serving: 4.3 g.
Net carbs per serving: 4.1 g.
Calories per serving: 238

WALNUT BLUE CHEESE BALL

¼ cup green onions, minced

1 clove garlic, minced

2 tbsp. celery, minced

2 tbsp. red bell pepper, chopped

½ tsp. sweet basil, chopped

1 tsp. Seafood Seasoning Mix (see p. 17)

2 tsp. Tabasco® Sauce

1 tbsp. Worcestershire sauce

2 8-oz. packages cream cheese, softened

½ cup blue cheese, crumbled

1 cup Swiss cheese, grated

1 cup colby cheese, grated

1 cup whole walnut halves

In a food processor put all the ingredients up to the cream cheese and blend at full power until well chopped and blended. Add the cream cheese and blend until smooth. Add the remaining ingredients except for the walnuts and blend until completely mixed. Scrape the mixture into a bowl and shape into a ball with your hands. Cover and store in the refrigerator for 2 hours. Remove and place in the center of a serving platter. Place walnuts on the ball so that all of it is covered. Serve chilled. Serves about 40.

Lagniappe: What a great cheese ball. This is easy, but the compliments will roll in. You can make this up to one week in advance and refrigerate. Put the walnuts on the ball and roll it in plastic wrap until ready to serve. Serve this with plenty of fresh cut vegetables, fruit, or low-carb crackers.

Carbs per serving: 1.1 g.

Net carbs per serving: .93 g.

Calories per serving: 85

CAJUN JACK CAKE

3 large eggs, slightly beaten
2 cups mayonnaise
2 tsp. Tabasco® Sauce
1 tsp. fresh ground black pepper
4 cups Monterey Jack cheese, shredded

1 cup sharp cheddar cheese, grated
½ cup Swiss cheese, grated
½ cup green onion bottoms, minced
1 clove garlic, finely minced

In a small mixing bowl, combine the eggs, mayonnaise, Tabasco® Sauce, and black pepper until smooth. In a large mixing bowl, add the remaining ingredients and mix them together well. Pour the egg/mayo mixture over the cheese mixture and blend together well. Pour into a lightly-greased, 1-quart spring form baking pan and bake at 325 degrees for 1 hour or until the egg has set. It should be nice and puffy but slightly firm. Remove from the oven and let it cool. Remove the spring pan ring when the cake as set. Slice thin and serve as an appetizer. Serves 15.

Lagniappe: Who says cheesecake is only for dessert? This is a great tasting appetizer that is excellent by itself or served with cut fruits or vegetables. It's a wonderful party food and great on a buffet table. Don't let anyone know it's low-carb until they taste it! Then you can tell them the carb count and how you can eat this and still be on a low-carb diet!

Carbs per serving: 2.4 g.
Net carbs per serving: 2.3 g.
Calories per serving: 536

TRAIL MIX

½ cup peanuts, salted

½ cup almonds, salted

½ cup cashews, salted

½ cup pecans, salted

1 cup of low-carb, high-fiber breakfast cereal

½ cup raisins

½ cup sugar-free chocolate candies

1 tsp. garlic powder

1 tsp. onion powder

½ tsp. cayenne pepper

½ tsp. salt

butter-flavored baking spray

Preheat the oven to 375 degrees. Mix all the nuts and cereal together in a mixing bowl. Pour onto a shallow, metal, non-stick baking dish and sprinkle with garlic powder, onion powder, cayenne pepper, and salt. Spray very lightly with butter-flavored baking spray. Bake for 7 minutes. Remove and let the mixture cool. Pour into a serving bowl. Add the raisins and candies and store until you are ready to serve as an appetizer or a wonderful trail mix. Serves 12.

Lagniappe: This recipe is really here to give you ideas. You can mix the low-carb snacks that you like and keep them stored for when you get the munchies. Being on a low-carb diet is not bad, because the philosophy that you work with is: When you are hungry . . . you eat! What a difference from other diets, where you deny yourself treats. All this diet requires is that you eat low-carb choices. Oh, the possibilities!

Carbs per serving: 12.2 g

Net carbs per serving: 7.1 g.

Calories per serving: 146

Gumbos, Stocks, and Soups

LOW-CARB SEAFOOD GUMBO

½ cup peanut oil
¼ cup all purpose flour
2 large onions, chopped
2 ribs celery, chopped
3 cloves garlic, minced
1 medium bell pepper, chopped
1 10-oz. can stewed tomatoes
3½ qt. Seafood Stock (see p. 89)
2½ tsp. Cajun Seasoning Mix (see p. 20)

2 tsp. Tabasco® Sauce
1½ tbsp. Worcestershire sauce
2 bay leaves
3 tsp. ThickenThin Not/Starch®
2 lbs. shrimp, peeled and deveined
1 lb. lump crabmeat
1 pint oysters
1 cup chopped green onions
½ cup finely minced parsley
filé powder to taste

Be sure all the prep work (chopping, peeling, mincing, etc.) is done ahead of time. Have all the ingredients lined up and ready for use. Heat a large, heavy stockpot or gumbo pot (at least 3 gallons) over high heat (be sure to use your highest efficiency burner). When the pot is hot, add the peanut oil. Just as it begins to smoke, add the flour, stirring constantly with a long wire whisk. Cook until the flour turns a dark reddish-brown, about 5 minutes if your heat is high enough. Take great care not to splash the mixture—it's very, very hot.

Stirring constantly, add the onions, celery, garlic, and bell peppers. Reduce the heat to medium-high and continue to stir constantly cooking for 3 more minutes. The temperature of the roux will drop dramatically, but it will still be quite hot. Stir in the tomatoes carefully and cook for 3 more minutes, stirring constantly. Add the stock and Cajun Seasoning Mix and stir in well. Continue to cook for 45 minutes, stirring often. The gumbo should begin to take on a nice, rich flavor. Add the Tabasco® Sauce, Worcestershire sauce, and bay leaves and cook for 15 more minutes.

Mix the thickener in a cup with liquid from the pot a little at a time until it has dissolved, then pour it into the gumbo pot and stir in well. Cook for 5 more minutes. Add the shrimp, crabmeat, and oysters, lower the heat to simmer, and cook for 12 more minutes, stirring occasionally. Finally, add the green onions and parsley and cook for 3 more minutes. Serve in large soup bowl. Season to taste with filé powder on top of each serving. Serve hot. Serves 10.

Lagniappe: It's hard to have a Cajun book of any kind without a gumbo recipe. This recipe is a genuine gumbo, but with much less flour in the roux. You get the true flavor of Cajun gumbo without all the carbs. I had to work on this recipe for a long time before I was satisfied. The ThickenThin Not/Starch® adds thickness to the gumbo, so the texture is closer to the real thing. To be perfectly honest, I like it just as well without the thickener, mainly because I like thin gumbo. Either way, it's great Cajun eating. You can use the same recipe to make Shrimp Gumbo by replacing all the seafood with 4 lbs. of shrimp and following the recipe as above. Or you can make Oyster Gumbo by substituting all the seafood above with 2 quarts of fresh oysters. You can also make Crawfish Gumbo by using 4 pounds of crawfish tails as the only seafood. Or you can make Crab Gumbo by using an additional pound of lump crabmeat and 2 dozen cleaned whole crabs as a substitute for the other seafood. When making crab gumbo, add the whole, cleaned crabs when you add the stock and the lump crabmeat when the other seafood is used. Gumbo is a wonderful part of Cajun heritage and no diet can stand to be without it.

You may not know that the word "gumbo" comes from the African word for okra. As you may notice, this gumbo does not have okra. The only essential elements of gumbo are a dark brown roux and filé powder. Filé powder is the ground up leaves of the sassafras tree. It gives gumbo its unique flavor. For those not used to filé, I would recommend eating just a sample at first then as you begin to enjoy the flavor add more to your liking. Filé should be added to the finished bowl of gumbo and not added to the pot. Cooking it tends to produce a unique bitter flavor that some like and some don't. This is genuine Cajun eating at it's best. Gumbos are well worth trying, even low-carb ones!

Carbs per serving: 12.3 g.
Net carbs per serving: 11.2 g.
Calories per serving: 210

CHICKEN AND ANDOUILLE GUMBO

½ cup peanut oil
¼ cup flour, all purpose
2 large onions, chopped
1 large bell pepper, chopped
2 stalks celery, minced
5 cloves garlic, minced
4 whole chicken breasts, (14 oz. each) cut in half and skin and bone removed
8 chicken thighs, skin removed (6 oz. each)
3 tsp. Cajun Seasoning Mix (see p. 20 for the recipe)
3½ qt. Chicken Stock (see p. 88 for the recipe) or chicken broth

2 tbsp. Worcestershire sauce
2 tsp. Tabasco® Sauce
1 tsp. onion powder
½ tsp. cayenne pepper
½ tsp. garlic powder
1 tsp. sweet basil
½ tsp. thyme
3 large bay leaves
1 lb. andouille sausage, sliced in circles about ¼-inch thick
1 tbsp. ThickenThin Not/Starch® thickener
1 cup green onions, finely chopped
½ cup fresh parsley, finely minced
filé powder to taste

In a very heavy gumbo pot or stockpot (at least 3 gallons), heat the oil over very high heat until hot. Add the flour and sauté, constantly stirring with a long heavy wire whisk. Cook over high heat until the roux becomes a dark brown. Be sure to constantly keep it moving to prevent sticking. It's the brown roux that imparts a great deal of flavor to the gumbo, so burning the roux will spoil the gumbo. When the dark color has been reached, add the onions, bell pepper, garlic, and celery and cook for 5 minutes, stirring constantly. Season the chicken with the Cajun Seasoning Mix until well seasoned. Add the seasoned chicken a little at a time. Cook the chicken for about 12 minutes, stirring constantly. Carefully add the stock, taking care not to splatter. Remember to keep everything constantly moving in the pot to prevent sticking in any spot. Add the Worcestershire sauce, Tabasco® Sauce, onion powder, cayenne, garlic powder, thyme, and bay leaves to the gumbo. Continue to cook until the gumbo starts to boil, then reduce the heat to simmer. Add the sausage and cook for 2 hours, stirring often.

Adjust seasonings to your individual taste. Mix the ThickenThin Not/Starch® with ½ cup of water in a small metal bowl, mixing well using a wire whisk. Add 1 cup of the hot gumbo to the bowl and mix together well, then pour it into the pot of gumbo. Stir well, then cook for 30 more minutes. The gumbo should thicken. Add the green onions and parsley and stir in well. Cook for 3 more minutes then serve in large bowls. Serve hot. Serves 12.

Lagniappe: This gumbo cooks a little quicker than the traditional gumbo because we are using chicken breasts and thighs and because we started with chicken stock. If you want to use water, use the whole chicken, still on the bone, chopped into serving pieces. If you want a really rich stock, use a rooster to make Rooster Gumbo. Use the recipe above, but have the rooster cut into serving pieces at the supermarket. It's easier to do it that way because the bones are hard to cut at home with a kitchen knife. They do it so much faster with the butcher saws. Instead of using just stock, add another quart of plain water when you add the stock and cook for 5 hours over simmering heat instead of the two hours the recipe calls for. Then remove the rooster from the pot, cook and debone it, chop it into bite-sized pieces, and return it to the pot. Cook for 20 more minutes, then add green onions and parsley and follow as above. This will taste like a different dish with the wonderful rich stock of the rooster. Because the meat is much more muscular, it takes a long time to soften it up. My grandmother always used to warn the mean roosters in the chicken yard to be nice or they'd be cooked in a big gumbo. She believed the meaner the rooster, the better the gumbo. I would never argue with her; I was afraid of what dish I'd end up in! The only other alternative that I'd recommend is making Chicken and Okra Gumbo. All you do is add 1½ pounds of cooked okra to the gumbo pot when you add the chicken. To cook the okra, just chop it, add ½ cups of onion, 3 tbsp. vegetable oil, 1 tsp. of salt and black pepper, and 1 tsp. of Tabasco® Sauce. Put it in an oven-proof, heavy pot that has a lid and put it in the oven at 375 degrees and cook for 30 minutes. Remove the lid, stir and return to the oven for 15 more minutes, then remove and add to the gumbo when you add the meat. This is a great way to make okra to serve as a side dish as well. So here you have three different gumbos and a dish of okra. Not bad for one recipe! Ça c'est beaucoup bon!

Carbs per serving: 7.6 g.
Net carbs per serving: 6.2 g.
Calories per serving: 732

ROUXLESS OKRA GUMBO

3 tbsp. peanut oil
2 lbs. fresh okra, sliced crosswise
3 tbsp. vegetable oil
6 medium onions, chopped
½ lb. ham, chopped
½ lb. smoked sausage, cut into circles

1 qt. Seafood Stock (see p. 89) or
  chicken broth
1 8-oz can tomato sauce
3 lbs. shrimp, (21-25's) peeled and
  deveined
4 whole cleaned crabs

In a medium heavy skillet, over medium-high heat, add the peanut oil and sauté the okra, stirring constantly until the okra begins to dry, about 40 minutes. The slime will be gone. In a large gumbo pot, add the vegetable oil and sauté the onions until they become clear. Add the ham and sausage and cook for 15 more minutes, stirring often. Add the okra, Seafood Stock, and tomato sauce and simmer for 20 minutes, stirring often over medium heat. Add the shrimp and crabs and cook for 15 more minutes, stirring often. Serve hot. Serves 10.

Lagniappe: This is a great gumbo, just not one we are very familiar with here in Cajun country. We usually make a dark brown roux, but when you are watching carbs, a roux is pretty much impossible. This is a great alternative. Instead of using flour to thicken the gumbo, the okra does the trick. Try it—you'll like it, especially when you are longing for the taste of good gumbo.

Carbs per serving: 16.8 g.
Net carbs per serving: 12.3 g.
Calories per serving: 430

BEEF STOCK

5 pounds beef soup meat
3 pounds of beef long ribs
1 gallon water
2 large onions, chopped
3 stalks celery, broken
4 carrots, broken
2 cloves garlic, crushed
3 bay leaves
2 tsp. whole black peppercorns

¼ bunch fresh parsley, with stems on
½ cup of green onion tops, chopped
½ medium turnip, chopped
2 tbsp. cabbage, chopped
1 tsp. salt
3 stems of fresh basil
2 sprigs of fresh thyme
1 tsp. Tabasco® Sauce

Preheat the oven to 500 degrees. Chop the soup meat into small pieces and set aside. Place the beef ribs in a shallow baking pan and bake for 20 minutes until they are quite brown, but not burned. Turn the ribs after 12 minutes. While the ribs are browning, sauté the soup meat over medium-high heat in a large stock pot or gumbo pot until the meat is nicely browned. Do not let the meat stick to the pot. When browned, add the water and bring to a hard boil. When the liquid is boiling, add the rest of the ingredients except for the ribs and reduce the heat to a low simmer. Add the ribs to the stockpot when they are finished browning. Simmer the stock for 5 to 6 hours. If the water level starts to drop, add a little more water and lower the heat a little.

Remove from the heat and let the stock cool. Strain the cooled broth from the meat and vegetable with a fine wire sieve. Put the broth in the refrigerator to chill. The fat should rise to the top and harden. Remove as much of the fat as possible. This should make about 2 quarts of stock. It may be eaten as is or used as the base for other soups or sauces.

Lagniappe: You can make this stock well ahead of the time you need it. It can be refrigerated for up to 5 days or frozen for later use. Let the stock thaw in the refrigerator and use as you would use any broth or stock. I like to freeze the stock in ice cub trays. When they are frozen I put them into plastic freezer bags for use as needed. I try to keep ¼ cup per cube so I can get the amount I need when a recipe calls for homemade stock.

This is an all-day project, but you should be able to make enough to last you for quite a while. There is no substitute for homemade stock. Purchased broth or stock might be acceptable, but it is not in the same league as homemade.

Don't throw away the leftover meat from the pot. Even though the bulk of the flavor is gone, the meat can be finely chopped and used to make sandwiches or to add meat flavor to a variety of dishes.

Carbs per one-cup serving: .1 g.
Net Carbs per one-cup serving: .1 g.
Calories per one-cup serving: 21

CHICKEN STOCK

6 pounds chicken wings, backs and legs

1 gallon water

2 medium onions, quartered

3 carrots, cut into thirds

3 stalks celery, chopped into thirds

½ bunch parsley, with stems on, but washed

2 cloves garlic, crushed

3 bay leaves

3 stems fresh basil

2 sprigs fresh thyme

15 whole black peppercorns

1 tsp. salt

2 whole cloves

1 tsp. Tabasco® Sauce

Preheat the oven to 500 degrees. Wash the chicken well in cold water. Remove as much skin as possible and place the chicken a shallow baking pan in the oven. Let the chicken brown nicely, turning after 10 minutes, then brown the other side for another 10 minutes. When done, remove from the heat and set aside. Add the remaining ingredients into a large stockpot or gumbo pot and bring to a hard boil, then reduce to a low simmer and add the chicken pieces to the pot. Simmer for 6 hours, stirring a few times. When done, remove the pot from the heat and let cool. When cool enough, strain with a fine sieve strainer. Cover the stock and refrigerate overnight. The next day, remove any fat that has floated to the top of the stockpot. This should make about 2 quarts of excellent stock.

Lagniappe: This may be eaten as a soup itself or used as a base for other soups and sauces. Homemade stock is hard to beat. Making stock is not really that hard; it just takes a lot of time. Make it on a day that you are doing something else away from the kitchen. You can either use it immediately, refrigerate it for up to 5 days, or freeze it. It freezes well. I like to freeze it in ice cube trays, putting ¼ cup liquid in each cube. When frozen, I put the cubes into plastic freezer bags and I have stock whenever I need it. To use, just thaw in the refrigerator and use as you would any broth or stock. This will add greatly to any soup or sauce you make.

Carbs per one-cup serving: .1 g.
Net Carbs per one-cup serving: .1 g.
Calories per one-cup serving: 23

SEAFOOD STOCK

Shells from 2 lbs. of shrimp

10 crab claws, cleaned (or 2 lobster shells if available)

1½ gallon water

2 stalks celery

2 carrots, each cut into four pieces

1 medium white onion, peeled and cut into fourths

3 garlic cloves, unpeeled and crushed

2 bay leaves

¼ bunch fresh parsley

4 green onions, washed and trimmed

1 tbsp. fresh turnip

10 black pepper corns

1 sprig of fresh sweet basil

1 sprig of fresh thyme

2 whole cloves

¼ tsp. mustard seeds

Place all the ingredients into a large stockpot. Bring to a boil over high heat, then reduce the heat to a simmer. Let the stock simmer for at least 4 hours, adding a cup of water at a time as the water begins to evaporate. Remove from the heat and let it cool for at least 30 minutes. Strain through a colander to remove the large pieces, then strain again through cheesecloth to remove the small pieces. Refrigerate for at least 1 hour. Makes about 3 cups of stock. This stock is used to enhance seafood dishes and is not really good enough to eat alone.

Lagniappe: This stock can be made well in advance and frozen for later use. I like to freeze it in ice cubes. Eight cubes equal about 1 cup of liquid. When frozen, I put them into plastic freezer bags to use as needed. It helps to make the stock when you have shrimp peeling and crab claws available. If I don't have both available at the same time, then I freeze the part I have until I have both. Stock can be refrigerated for up to 4 days. The taste really intensifies as it sits in the refrigerator, so you are actually improving the quality. It is an extra effort to make your own stock. It will add so much flavor to your dish, and the people you are cooking for will know that you care!

Carbs per one-cup serving: .1 g.
Net Carbs per one-cup serving: .1 g.
Calories per one-cup serving: 17

BOUILLABAISSE

1 cup of extra virgin olive oil

1 large onion, chopped

½ cup celery minced

1 leek, cut into julienne pieces about 1½-inches long

1 carrot, julienned about 1½-inches long

3 cloves garlic, minced

3 cups of peeled and diced tomatoes

1 tbsp. tomato paste

2 tsp. Tabasco® Sauce

1 cup dry white wine

3 qt. Seafood Stock (see p. 89 for recipe)

½ tsp. saffron

1½ tsp. salt

1½ tsp. fresh ground black pepper

1 16-oz. lobster tail with shell on and cut into 8 pieces

1½ lb. large (15-20's) shrimp tails, with shells on

1 lb. sea scallops

25 medium-sized clams, cleaned

1½ lb. mussels, medium size and cleaned

1 lb. fresh redfish fillet, cut into large cubes

½ cup Pernod liqueur

½ cup fresh parsley, minced

In a large stockpot over medium-high heat, add half the olive oil and let it get hot. Add the onion, celery, leeks, carrot, and garlic and sauté for 10 minutes. Add the tomatoes and tomato paste; cook for 5 minutes, stirring often. Add the Tabasco® Sauce, wine, Seafood Stock, saffron, salt, and pepper and cook for 15 more minutes. In another large, heavy saucepan, add the remaining half of the olive oil and let it get hot. Sauté the lobster, shrimp, and scallops for 7 minutes, then add them to the stockpot with the vegetables; stir and cover. Sauté the clams, mussels, and redfish for 10 minutes in the remaining olive oil. Then carefully pour the clams-fish mixture into the stockpot, taking care not to splash yourself with the hot oil. Bring the bouillabaisse to a boil and cook for 3 minutes, then lower the heat to a simmer. Add the Pernod and fresh parsley and cook for 3 more minutes. Serve immediately. Serves 8.

Lagniappe: This is quite a dish! It's the kind of soup you serve as a meal for company. You almost buy out the seafood shop to make this soup, but the flavor and taste is divine. You are sure to get raves. You should not make this in advance because the seafood begins to lose its quality when it is refrigerated. It has a lot of ingredients, but it's not really difficult to make. You can chop everything in advance and have it ready to cook. A nice green salad is all you need for a great meal. Enjoy!

Carbs per serving 13.9 g.
Net carbs per serving: 12.3 g.
Calories per serving: 652

LUMP CRABMEAT SOUP

¼ cup unsalted butter
1 shallot, minced
2 cloves garlic, minced
¼ cup green onions, minced
2 tbsp. bell pepper, minced
2 tbsp. celery, minced
1 tbsp. soy flour

1 cup Seafood Stock (see p. 89) or
   chicken broth
1 cup heavy whipping cream
1 tsp. Seafood Seasoning Mix (see p. 17)
1 pound lump crabmeat
¼ cup fresh parsley, minced
1 tsp. fresh basil, minced

In a medium saucepan over medium heat, add the butter and let it melt and get hot. Add the shallot, garlic, green onions, bell pepper and celery and sauté for 5 minutes, stirring constantly. Add the soy flour, blend it in, and cook for 1 minute. Reduce the heat to low and add the Seafood Stock and cream. Heat until it starts to thicken. Add the Seafood Seasoning Mix and crabmeat. Stir well until the crabmeat is hot and steam starts to rise from the pot. Add the parsley and basil and heat for 1 more minute. Serve immediately. Serves 4.

Lagniappe: This is a quick and easy recipe that yields tons of praise. This soup is light and rich at the same time. Almost anything you do with lump crabmeat is delicious. This soup can be made in advance and refrigerated. To reheat, just heat on low, stirring gently, then serve. Take care not to stir it so vigorously that you break the wonderful lumps of crabmeat. You can't really freeze this soup. It loses too much texture and quality. You can use frozen lump crabmeat, but fresh is always best!

Carbs per serving: 5.3 g.
Net Carbs per serving: 4.3 g.
Calories per serving: 438

SHRIMP AND ASPARAGUS BISQUE

3 tbsp. unsalted butter

1 cup green onions, chopped

2 cloves garlic, minced

1 cup fresh mushrooms, sliced

2 cups of tender young asparagus

¼ cup celery

¼ cup red bell pepper, diced

3 tbsp. soy flour

1 tsp. Seafood Seasoning Mix (see p. 17)

1 lb. shrimp (41-50's), peeled and deveined

1 tsp. fresh basil, minced

1 bay leaf

1 tsp. Tabasco® Sauce

1 cup heavy whipping cream

2 cups half-and-half

2 cups of Seafood Stock (see p. 89) or chicken broth

1 cup Monterey Jack cheese, shredded

½ cup Swiss cheese, shredded

In a large saucepan over medium-high heat, melt the butter and let it get hot. Sauté the onions, garlic, mushrooms, asparagus, celery, and red pepper for 10 minutes or until tender. Blend in the flour and cook, stirring constantly for 3 minutes. Season the shrimp with the seasoning mix and add to the saucepan. Sauté for 5 more minutes, stirring often. Add all the remaining ingredients except for the cheese and let the soup almost come to a boil. Do not let it boil. Add the cheese and stir until the cheese is melted and the soup is steamy and hot but not boiling. Serve hot. Serves 6.

Lagniappe: This is a full-bodied soup. It can be served not just as an appetizer, but as a meal. It fills you up but is not so heavy that it stays with you. You can make the soup completely in advance and store in the refrigerator. It actually will improve the taste to refrigerate. The flavors do a better job of blending when sitting in the refrigerator. To reheat, just put in a saucepan and heat over low heat until the soup is hot.

Carbs per serving: 8.6 g.

Net carbs per serving: 6.2 g.

Calories per serving: 428

OYSTER SOUP

1 qt. fresh oysters
3 cups half-and-half
1 cup heavy whipping cream
1 tsp. Seafood Seasoning Mix (see
   p. 17)

1 tsp. fresh sweet basil, minced
¼ cup celery, minced
¼ cup fresh parsley, minced
¼ cup unsalted butter

Drain the oysters from their liquid and place the liquid in a medium saucepan over medium heat. Put the half-and-half and the whipping cream in another medium saucepan and set aside. Add the remaining ingredients to the oyster liquid and bring it to a hard boil, then reduce the heat to simmer. Slowly add the two creams to the hot oyster liquid until all is added. Let the mixture get hot, then add the oysters, taking care not to bring the oysters to a boil, just a simmer. Let the oysters simmer until they are puffy and the edges curl up. Serve immediately. Serves 6.

Lagniappe: You might look at this recipe and think, I don't think so! Well, you would be wrong. This is heavenly eating. The liquid is out of this world. This soup is so good that you'll be hard-pressed not to lick the bowl when you're finished. Sometimes simple cooking can be excellent!

Carbs per serving: 9.9 g.
Net carbs per serving: 9.8 g.
Calories per serving: 396

BROCCOLI SOUP DIVINE

2 tbsp. unsalted butter

½ cup onions, chopped

¼ cup celery, chopped

1 clove garlic, minced

1 10-oz. package frozen broccoli spears, thawed and chopped

1 cup half-and-half

3 oz. American cheese, cut in small blocks

1 cup Swiss cheese, grated

¼ cup fresh parsley, minced

½ tsp. fresh basil, minced

½ tsp. salt

½ tsp. fresh ground black pepper

1 tsp. Tabasco® Sauce

In a small, heavy skillet over medium-high heat, add the butter and let it melt. When the butter is hot, add the onions, celery, and garlic and sauté for 4 minutes. Add the broccoli and sauté for 2 more minutes. Put the mixture into a blender and blend completely. In a medium-sized saucepan over medium heat, add the cream and the blended broccoli and vegetables. Let the mixture start to get hot, but not boil. Add the remaining ingredients and let the soup just start to boil, then reduce the heat, stirring constantly. The soup should be thick and creamy. Serve hot. Serves 4.

Lagniappe: This is a quick and outstanding soup. It's easy to make and the taste is beyond belief. If you like your broccoli to be in large pieces, don't put the broccoli in the blender or put half in the blender and half in the pot. I like to cut the stems and put them in the blender and leave the flowerets whole for the soup. However you serve it, it's great!

Carbs per serving: 11 g.
Net carbs per serving: 7.1 g.
Calories per serving: 433

POTAGE AU CHOUX

3 tbsp. extra virgin olive oil
5 cups chopped cabbage
1 large onion, chopped
2 cloves garlic, minced
½ cup celery, sliced
1 cup boneless ham, cut into chunks

1 tsp. Beef Seasoning Mix (see p. 19)
1 tsp. Tabasco® Sauce
2 cups Beef Stock (see p. 86)
½ tsp. fresh sweet basil, minced
1½ cups Swiss cheese, grated

In a large saucepan over medium-high heat, add the olive oil and let it get hot. Add the cabbage, onion, garlic and celery and sauté for 3 minutes. Add the ham and Beef Seasoning Mix and sauté for 10 more minutes, stirring often. The cabbage should be slightly browned and clear. Add the remaining ingredients except the cheese and bring to a boil, then reduce the heat to simmer and let the soup cook for 20 minutes. Add the cheese and stir it through and serve. Serves 6.

Lagniappe: This is a nice soup that you can serve as a meal or with a few Ham Roll-ups (see p. 66). It is good in the summer or nice in cool weather as well. It can be made in advance and refrigerated until you are ready to serve; just don't add the cheese until right before serving. I also like this soup with a Cajun Low-Carb Sandwich (see p. 209).

Carbs per serving: 8.6 g.
Net Carbs per serving: 5.4 g.
Calories per serving: 337

SPINACH SOUP TO DIE FOR

2 tbsp. extra virgin olive oil
2 tbsp. shallots, chopped
¼ cup celery, chopped
¼ cup green onions, minced
1 clove garlic, minced
1 10-oz. package frozen spinach, thawed
1 cup heavy whipping cream
1 cup Chicken Stock (see p. 88) or chicken broth

1 cup Monterey Jack cheese, grated
1 cup Provolone cheese, grated
¼ cup American cheese, grated
¼ cup fresh parsley, minced
½ tsp. fresh basil, minced
½ tsp. salt
½ tsp. fresh ground black pepper
1 tsp. Tabasco® Sauce

In a small, heavy skillet over medium-high heat, add the oil let it get hot. When the oil starts to pop, add the shallots, celery, green onions, and garlic and sauté for 4 minutes. Put the vegetable mixture into a blender along with the spinach and blend completely. In a large sauce pot over medium heat, add the cream and the blended spinach and vegetables. Let the mixture start to get hot, but not boil. Add the remaining ingredients and let the soup just start to boil, then reduce the heat to low, stirring constantly. The soup should be thick and creamy. Serve hot. Serves 4.

Lagniappe: This is another quick and easy soup. It's easy to make and the taste is beyond belief. This is a nice accompaniment to almost any meal. It can also act as a sauce for chicken breast or pork chops. Just spoon about ¼ cup of the soup over the meat and serve. It will look elegant and the taste-well, you be the judge!

Carbs per serving: 11.7 g.
Net carbs per serving: 11 g.
Calories per serving: 813

BRIE CHEESE SOUP

3 tbsp. unsalted butter
½ cup onions, finely chopped
½ cup celery, minced
2 tbsp. carrots, minced
1 clove garlic, minced
2 tbsp. soy flour
1 cup Chicken Stock (see p. 88) or
    chicken broth

1 tsp. fresh sweet basil, minced
⅛ tsp. thyme
1 cup heavy whipping cream
8 oz. Brie cheese
2 tbsp. fresh parsley, minced

In a medium saucepan over medium heat, add the butter and let it melt and get hot. When hot, add the onions, celery, carrots, and garlic and sauté for 5 minutes, stirring constantly. Add the soy flour land blend in well and continue cooking over medium heat for 1 minute, then add the stock, fresh basil, and thyme. Reduce the heat to low and continue to cook until the soup starts to thicken, about 3 minutes. Slowly add the cream, stirring constantly as you add. Cut the hard rind off the Brie and chop the cheese into cubes. Add to the pot, stirring often until all the cheese has melted and thickens nicely. Add the parsley and stir through. Serve hot. Serves 4.

Lagniappe: This is a soup to remember. It's simple, yet the taste of Brie comes through so well. It's a nice way to start out any meal, but it's also great by itself. I like to eat it with a roll-up sandwich. You can completely make it in advance and refrigerate until you are ready to serve. It keeps nicely in the refrigerator for 3 or 4 days.

Carbs per serving: 6.1 g.
Net carbs per serving: 4.2 g.
Calories per serving: 527

SUMMER SQUASH SOUP

2 tbsp. clarified unsalted butter

2 tbsp. celery, minced

1 medium onion, chopped

3 tbsp. Bechamel Sauce (see p. 26)

2 cups Chicken Stock (see p. 88) or chicken broth

5 cups yellow summer squash, cleaned and cut in circles (skin on)

1 tsp. Tabasco® Sauce

1 tsp. salt

1 tsp. fresh ground black pepper

1 packet of Splenda® sweetener

2 tsp. Worcestershire sauce

½ cup heavy whipping cream

½ tsp. nutmeg

2 tbsp. green onions, finely chopped, for garnish

2 tbsp. parsley, finely minced, for garnish

In a medium saucepan over medium-high heat, add the clarified butter. When it gets hot, add the celery and onions. Sauté for 5 minutes, stirring often. Add the Bechamel Sauce and blend it in, then set aside for later use. Add the chicken stock into a large stockpot and bring to a boil. Let it boil for 5 minutes, uncovered. Add the squash and cook in the stock for 7 minutes at a hard boil. Reserve the liquid from the squash for later use. Remove the squash from the pot and place in a blender with all the remaining ingredients except for the green onions and parsley. Blend at high speed until the squash is well pureed. Pour into a large saucepan over medium heat and bring the mixture to a low boil. When it begins to boil, blend in the sautéed vegetables and stir together well. Add ¼ cup of stock from the pot you boiled the squash in until you get the consistency of the soup that you like. Garnish with chopped green onions and parsley and serve hot. Serves 4.

Lagniappe: This is a wonderful summer soup. It has the light flavors of summer. You can make this soup completely in advance and refrigerate until you are ready to serve. Just heat it over medium heat until hot and garnish with the green onions and parsley and serve.

Carbs per serving: 6.4 g.
Net carbs per serving: 4.2 g.
Calories per serving: 108

CREAM OF ALMOND SOUP

1 cup blanched almonds, chopped
1 large onion, peeled and whole
2 whole cloves
2 cloves of garlic, crushed but still in its paper shell
3 cups of Chicken Stock (see p. 88)
1 bay leaf
2 tbsp. butter

1 tbsp. all-purpose flour
1 tbsp. soy flour
½ cup half-and-half
1 cup heavy whipping cream
1 tsp. Tabasco® Sauce
⅛ cup sliced toasted almonds for garnish
1 tsp. fresh chives, finely chopped

Stick the two cloves of garlic into the onion. Combine the almonds, onion with the two cloves stuck in it, garlic, chicken stock, and bay leaf in a medium saucepan. Simmer covered for 45 minutes. When finished, discard the onion and bay leaf and set the broth aside to cool. In another medium saucepan over medium-high heat, melt the butter and let get hot. When it is hot, add the soy flour and the all-purpose flour and blend into the butter thoroughly. Cook for 3 minutes, then gradually add the half-and-half. Stir constantly until smooth and thickened. Combine the cream mixture with the chicken-almond stock. Remove from the heat and stir in the heavy cream and Tabasco® Sauce. Heat over low heat, stirring constantly. Do not bring to a boil. Serve with the slivered toasted almonds and chives on top. Serve warm. Serves 6.

Lagniappe: This is a wonderful cream soup. It is not your usual soup, but it's one that is full of flavor. You can make this soup completely in advance and store in the refrigerator. Just hold the sliced almonds and chives until right before you are ready to serve. To heat, put in a saucepan over low heat, stirring often, until it is hot enough to serve. You might wonder why you stuck the cloves into the onion. The onion juice helps to carry the flavor of the cloves throughout the onion and into the soup stock. It's a nice, savory trick. It produces a unique flavor that you don't get from just boiling them separately.

Carbs per serving: 12.8 g.
Net carbs per serving: 8.3 g.
Calories per serving: 386

Salads and Salad Dressings

CRAB SALAD DON LOUIS

1 cup of mayonnaise

1 tbsp. horseradish, prepared

2 packets of Splenda®

2 tbsp. low-carb chili sauce (no sugar)

3 tbsp. lemon juice, fresh

1½ cups fresh mushrooms, sliced

1 cup canned artichoke hearts, cut into thirds and drained

1 avocado, peeled and cut into cubes

½ cup of celery, sliced

½ fresh Bosc pear, peeled and cut into cubes

1 lb. lump crabmeat

6 tomatoes

6 hard boiled eggs, quartered

Cut the tomatoes lengthwise into six wedges, but do not cut all the way through the tomato to the bottom. It should form a star. In a large mixing bowl, combine the mayonnaise, horseradish, Splenda®, chili sauce, and lemon juice until well blended. Fold the mushrooms, artichoke, avocado, celery, and pear into the dressing mix. When well coated, gently fold in the crabmeat, taking care not to break apart the nice lump pieces. Arrange a huge mound of crabmeat salad into the center of each tomato until all the crab mixture is used. Decorate the plate with 4 wedges of egg each. Sprinkle with paprika and serve. Serves 6.

Lagniappe: While this is in the salad section, it's really a complete meal in itself. It would really be difficult for someone to eat this salad and go on to a regular dinner. Crabmeat is so rich and all the added items make this a salad to remember. You can make this salad up to 24 hours in advance and just put on the tomato and set the plate up when you are ready to serve. It actually improves the flavor to make the mixture in advance and let it stand in the refrigerator. This salad is an award-winner!

Carbs per serving: 16.1 g.
Net carbs per serving: 12 g.
Calories per serving: 524

SHRIMP AND MUSHROOM SALAD

1 clove garlic
2 green onions, finely chopped
2 tbsp. red bell pepper, diced
2 cups mushrooms, sliced
2 cups (8 oz.) boiled shrimp, chopped
 coarsely

2 tbsp. extra virgin olive oil
¼ cup mayonnaise
2 tbsp. lemon juice, fresh
1 tsp. Tabasco® Sauce
1 tsp. fresh basil, minced
salt and black pepper to taste

In a large salad bowl, add the garlic and green onions; mix together and crush the garlic and onions into the side of the bowl with a heavy spoon. Add the bell pepper, mushrooms, and shrimp and toss until well mixed. In a small mixing bowl, add the remaining ingredients (except for the salt, pepper, and lettuce) and whip it together well using a wire whisk until well mixed. Salt and pepper to taste and add the shrimp and mushrooms and mix well. Spoon the dressing mix over the shrimp and blend together well. Divide the lettuce equally on 4 salad plates. Spoon the shrimp mixture equally on top of the lettuce and serve immediately. Serves 4.

Lagniappe: What a great seafood salad. It's easy and quick. I like to make this dish the day after I've had a shrimp boil so I can use the left-over shrimp. You can make it completely in advance and refrigerate until you are ready to serve. This also makes a nice appetizer. Just don't call it a salad in that case—call it a shrimp appetizer! Either way, it's delicious!

Carbs per serving: 3.9 g.
Net carbs per serving: 3.1 g.
Calories per serving: 237

CRAWFISH SALAD

2½ cups crawfish tails, cooked, peeled and chopped
½ cup celery, chopped
½ cup green onions, chopped
¼ cup red bell pepper, diced
2 hard boiled eggs, chopped
1 tsp. Tabasco® Sauce

1 tsp. Worcestershire sauce
½ tsp. fresh ground black pepper
1 tsp. salt
½ cup mayonnaise
1 tbsp. sweet pickle relish
½ cup dill pickle, finely chopped

Combine all the ingredients together and mix until well blended. Place in the refrigerator for 2 hours. Serve chilled. Serves 4.

Lagniappe: This salad is a great way to use left over crawfish from a crawfish boil. It can be made up to two days in advance. Just store tightly covered in the refrigerator. This salad can also be used as an appetizer. I like to serve the crawfish on top of a bed of shredded lettuce.

Carbs per serving: 2.7 g.
Net carbs per serving: 2.1 g.
Calories per serving: 252

CARROT AND CELERY SALAD

2¼ cups carrot, grated
1¼ cups celery, sliced thin
¼ cup green onion, bottoms
1 tsp. Tabasco® Sauce

1 packet Equal® sweetener
1 tsp. balsamic vinegar
2 tbsp. parsley, finely minced
½ cup mayonnaise

Mix all the ingredients together in a mixing bowl and refrigerate for 1 hour. Serve chilled. Serves 6.

Lagniappe: What ease, what taste, what praise! All true of this simple salad. It will please your guests and they won't believe it was so easy. You can make it in advance and store for up to 4 days before serving. Even though Atkins suggests not using balsamic vinegar, don't use a substitute. It is critical to the taste of the salad, and it is just one teaspoon. The recipe needs the intense flavor of the vinegar.

Carbs per serving: 9.1 g.
Net carbs per serving: 6.8 g.
Calories per serving: 98

CHILLED TOMATO SALAD

3 cups tomatoes, chopped (skin left on)
3 cups cucumbers, cut into ⅓-inch
   slices then quartered
½ cup celery, chopped
½ cup bell pepper, diced
½ cup onions, chopped
1 clove garlic, finely minced

1 tbsp. balsamic vinegar
⅓ cup red wine vinegar
1 tsp. Tabasco® Sauce
1 tsp. salt
1 tsp. black pepper
2 tbsp. Splenda® sweetener
½ tsp. fresh basil, minced

In a large mixing bowl, add all the ingredients and stir together well. Refrigerate tightly covered for 1 hour. Serve chilled. Serves 6.

Lagniappe: This is a great salad to serve with almost any meal. I like to just keep it in the refrigerator for a quick snack. It takes care of hunger pains that might strike at any time, day or night. It is a good way to have a low-carb, healthy snack around to combat cravings. It will keep in the refrigerator for 3 or 4 days. The vinegar loses a bit of its potency, but the vegetables start to get a little pickled taste. See the note about balsamic vinegar on page 53.

Carbs per serving: 8.6 g.
Net carbs per serving: 6.4 g.
Calories per serving: 45

JUST TOMATO SALAD

6 large tomatoes
1 tbsp. fresh basil, minced
salt and pepper to taste
3 tbsp. extra virgin olive oil
½ cup onion, finely grated

1 tbsp. celery, finely minced
1 tsp. Tabasco® Sauce
1 tbsp. balsamic vinegar
1 tsp. Dijon mustard
1 tbsp. chives, finely minced

Slice the tomatoes and arrange in a single layer on a large, flat platter. Sprinkle evenly with the fresh basil and salt and pepper to taste. In a small mixing bowl, combine the remaining ingredients with a wire whisk until well blended then drizzle over the tomatoes. Serve immediately. Serves 6.

Lagniappe: This is an easy salad and one that brings raves because of the fresh tomatoes. Sometimes simple is good! You can cut the tomatoes in advance and sprinkle with basil, salt, and pepper, then cover with plastic wrap until you are ready to serve. You can also mix the dressing in advance and store covered in the refrigerator until ready to serve. Do not put the dressing on the tomatoes in advance of serving time. You can leave the dressing covered in the refrigerator for up to 3 days. Don't cut the tomatoes more than 3 hours in advance. See the note about balsamic vinegar on page 53.

Carbs per serving: 8.6 g.
Net carbs per serving: 7.1 g.
Calories per serving: 50

FRESH OKRA AND TOMATO MARINATE

3 cups fresh okra
water to cover
2 tsp. salt
¼ cup of white distilled vinegar
2 medium tomatoes, cut into 10 slices,
   each lengthwise

1 cup fresh mushrooms, sliced
⅔ cup Italian salad dressing
salt and pepper to taste
4 cups lettuce

Put the okra in a large pot and cover with water. Add the salt and vinegar and bring the okra to a boil for 20 minutes. Remove from the heat, drain the okra and let it cool. In a large mixing bowl add the remaining ingredients except for the lettuce and the salt and pepper and stir together until well coated. Add the okra and again stir together well. Cover and refrigerate overnight. When you are ready to serve, salt and pepper to taste and serve over the lettuce. Serves 6.

Lagniappe: This is a salad that you can really get to know. The okra becomes somewhat pickled and is at its peak. This is great with any meal, but it is perfect with a nice piece of meat or chicken. You can make it in advance and refrigerate for up to 3 days. This is a great crowd-pleaser.

Carbs per serving: 9.9 g.
Net carbs per serving: 6.7 g
Calories per serving: 90

ARTICHOKE AND TOMATO SALAD

1 16-oz. can artichoke hearts, well drained and cut in half

2 medium tomatoes, sliced into 6 wedges each

¼ cup celery, sliced

½ cup Italian dressing

1 tbsp. balsamic vinegar

1 tsp. Tabasco® Sauce

4 cups of lettuce, torn

Mix together the artichoke hearts, tomatoes, and celery in a mixing bowl that has a lid. Add the Italian dressing, vinegar, and Tabasco® Sauce and mix together well. Refrigerate over night, stirring a few times. When you are ready to serve, tear the lettuce and put into a salad bowl. Add the artichokes and tomatoes and about half of the marinating liquid. Toss together well and serve immediately. Serves 6.

Lagniappe: This couldn't be easier. You can make it in advance and store for up to 3 days. After that the tomatoes really do start to fall apart. It makes a wonderful salad to bring to a buffet or covered dish. It'll look like you really worked hard, but you'll know it's only the great flavors that were working. See the note about balsamic vinegar on page 53.

Carbs per serving: 7.9 g.
Net carbs per serving: 6.3 g.
Calories per serving: 102

CAJUN COLE SLAW

4 cups green cabbage, shredded
2 cups purple cabbage, shredded
½ cup carrots, shredded
¼ cup green onions, finely chopped
¾ cup mayonnaise
¼ cup sour cream

3 packages Equal® sweetener
2 tbsp. red wine vinegar
1 tsp. Tabasco® Sauce
½ tsp. salt
1 tsp. fresh ground black pepper

Mix together the first four ingredients in a large mixing bowl until well blended. In a small mixing bowl, mix together the remaining ingredients until well blended. Pour the small bowl into the large bowl, stirring well to make sure all the vegetables are coated. Cover and chill for 1 hour in the refrigerator. Serve chilled. Serves 6.

Lagniappe: This slaw keeps well in the refrigerator for up to 3 days. It has a tendency to get a little stronger onion flavor when you leave it stored, but the taste is still wonderful. This slaw is great as a side dish for almost any meal.

Carbs per serving: 6.4 g.
Net carbs per serving: 4.2 g.
Calories per serving: 68

SALAD AVOCADO

2 large avocados, peeled and chopped
2 cups of cherry tomatoes, halved
½ head lettuce, sliced
1 cup purple cabbage, sliced
2 tbsp. lime juice

5 whole large black olives, sliced
1 tbsp. chili powder
1 tsp. Tabasco® Sauce
½ cup Thousand Island Dressing (see p. 120 for recipe)

In a large mixing bowl, mix together all the ingredients until well blended. Take care to make sure all is well blended. Chill for 1 hour. Serves 6.

Lagniappe: This is a great salad with almost any meal. It's easy and the flavor is super. It will keep in the refrigerator for up to 3 days. When I leave it for more than a day, I add another teaspoon of lime juice. It helps keep the avocado fresh and green.

Carbs per serving: 12.4 g.
Net carbs per serving: 6.7 g.
Calories per serving: 237

FRESH SPINACH SALAD

6 cups fresh spinach, washed and
   separated
4 hard boiled eggs, sliced into circles
12 slices bacon, cooked and crumbled
1 green onion, cut into thirds and
   sliced very thin

2 cups Spinach Salad Dressing
   Euphemie (see p. 123)
1 cup fresh mushrooms, sliced
1 tsp. Tabasco® Sauce
salt and pepper to taste

Toss all the ingredients together, mixing until the spinach is well coated with dressing. Serve immediately. Serves 6.

Lagniappe: This is a wonderful spinach salad. It's simple to make, but elegant. You can make the salad in advance and add the dressing just before you are ready to serve. Spinach makes a wonderful salad. While the carb count for this salad is really low, the calorie count is high. You can cut down the calories by using less dressing. If you cut the dressing to 1 cup, which will still coat the spinach, you cut the calorie count in half. It might be somewhat inflated anyway, since most people don't lick the plate and drink all their dressing. So I say, just make it this way once and then determine how much dressing you like.

Carbs per serving: 2.8 g.
Net carbs per serving: 1.7 g.
Calories per serving: 675

CAULIFLOWER SALAD ACADIE

4 cups cauliflower florets
water to cover
2 tsp. salt
2 tsp. whole black peppercorns
1 cup mayonnaise

1 tbsp. extra virgin olive oil
¼ cup Creole mustard
1 tsp. Tabasco® Sauce
½ tsp. fresh basil, finely chopped

Wash the cauliflower florets in cold water and place them in a large pot; cover with water and add the salt and black pepper corns. Bring to a boil and cook until the cauliflower is tender, about 7 minutes. Take care not to overcook. Remove from the water immediately and drain. Place in a large mixing bowl, cover and chill for 2 hours. In a small mixing bowl add the remaining ingredients and blend together well. Cover and chill until ready to serve the salad. When ready to serve, mix the dressing with the drained cauliflower until the cauliflower is well coated. Serve chilled. Serves 6.

Lagniappe: This is a salad that will please your palate and is different enough to spark comments. You can make this up to 2 days in advance and refrigerate until you are ready to serve. I do not like to mix the dressing with the cauliflower until I am ready to serve because it keeps the flavors separate and adds to the taste and texture. This is a wonderful buffet salad and a great salad to take to a covered dish.

Carbs per serving: 4.7 g.
Net carbs per serving: 2.9 g.
Calories per serving: 310

MARDI GRAS SALAD

1 cup petit pois peas, drained
1½ cup green beans, drained
½ cup red bell pepper, diced
½ cup green bell pepper, diced
1 cup mushrooms, sliced
½ cup onions, finely chopped
1 cup celery, sliced thin

½ cup Splenda® sweetener
½ cup distilled white vinegar
½ cup vegetable oil
1 tsp. salt
1 tsp. black pepper, finely ground
1 tsp. Tabasco® Sauce
1 tsp. paprika

Mix all ingredients together in a large mixing bowl that has a cover and let it stand and marinate for 24 hours in the refrigerator. Stir the mixture at least 3 times during the marinating time. Serve chilled. Serves 8.

Lagniappe: This is a different salad, but one that's sure to please. You can make this up to 4 days in advance. The flavor will actually improve while it sits in the refrigerator. This is a great salad to take to a covered dish or a buffet. I like to keep it in the refrigerator for a snack food. It's got lots of fiber and will kill your hunger pains. Because the fiber is high in this dish, the net carbs are almost half of the total carb count. This is a great dish for those who want to add fiber to their diet.

Carbs per serving: 9.2 g.
Net carbs per serving: 5.8 g.
Calories per serving: 169

KIDNEY BEAN SALAD

2 15¼-oz. cans dark red kidney beans, drained
½ cup celery, chopped
½ cup red bell pepper, diced
1 cup onions, chopped
½ cup dill pickle, chopped
½ lb. sharp cheddar cheese, cut into small blocks

½ lb. ham, cut into strips
2 hard boiled eggs, sliced
1 tsp. Tabasco® Sauce
1 tsp. salt
1 tsp. balsamic vinegar
1 cup mayonnaise
6 cups lettuce, shredded

In a large mixing bowl, mix together all the ingredients except the lettuce until thoroughly blended. Chill for at least 3 hours before serving. When ready to serve, spread the lettuce evenly on six salad plates and evenly spoon out the bean salad on top. Serve immediately. Serves 6.

Lagniappe: This is a salad or a meal. It's your choice. It is hearty enough to serve a main dish, but it's still a salad. It serves 8 as a salad and as a main dish. You can completely make it in advance and refrigerate for up to 3 days before serving. This is a great salad for a buffet or a covered dish. While this has a little higher carb count, it is loaded with fiber. You can use the same recipe to make Black Bean Salad by substituting black beans for the kidney beans and following the recipe as above. The carb count is almost identical, but the black beans have a bit more fiber. Since you only use 1 teaspoon of the balsamic vinegar, I don't recommend substituting another vinegar. The small amount goes a long way to making this recipe exciting, even though Atkins® urges you to make other choices.

Carbs per serving: 12.5 g.
Net carbs per serving: 8 g.
Calories per serving: 547

FRUIT SALAD ETIENNE

1 3-oz. package lime-flavored, sugar-free gelatin
1 cup boiling water
¼ cup Splenda® sweetener
1 cup small-curd cottage cheese (4 percent fat)
1 cup celery, chopped
2 tbsp. red bell pepper, diced

½ cup pecans, chopped
1 cup fresh pineapple, cut into chunks
1 cup fresh strawberries, chopped
½ 4 oz. package cream cheese, softened
1 tbsp. lemon juice
3 tbsp. mayonnaise
6 cup lettuce, shredded

Dissolve the gelatin in boiling water. Add the Splenda® and let the gelatin cool until it begins to thicken and becomes syrupy. When cooled, stir in the cottage cheese, celery, red bell pepper, and pecans until well blended. Fold in the pineapple and strawberries until well mixed. Line a cake pan with wax paper and pour the gelatin mixture into the pan. Chill in the refrigerator until firm. Make a frosting with the cream cheese, lemon juice, and mayonnaise by beating it together until it is smooth and creamy. Turn the jell out of the cake pan when it is solid and spread the frosting on top of the gelatin. Place about a cup of shredded lettuce on each salad plate. Cut the gelatin into 6 even wedges and place on top of the lettuce. Serve immediately. Serves 6.

Lagniappe: This is company salad. It is a wonderful salad that is almost a dessert. You can completely make this in advance and store until you are ready to cut and spread the frosting. This is a great way to serve fruit and have a salad at the same time.

Carbs per serving: 10.9 g.
Net carbs per serving: 7.7 g.
Calories per serving: 285

PINK SALAD DUPUIS

1 0.3-oz. box sugar-free strawberry gelatin
½ cup boiling water
½ cup Splenda® sweetener
1 cup raspberries, washed in cold water and drained

½ cup fresh pineapple, chopped into small chunks
1 cup cottage cheese (4 percent fat)
1 8-oz. container Cool Whip®, defrosted
¼ cup pecans, chopped

In a glass bowl, add the gelatin and pour the boiling water over it. Stir until the gelatin is dissolved. Add the Splenda® and blend it in until dissolved. Refrigerate for 20 minutes and let it start to gel. Put the remaining ingredients into the bowl and stir them through until well mixed. Pour into 6 lightly-greased individual gelatin molds and place in the refrigerator until the mold is set, about 5 hours. Remove the mold and serve as a chilled jelled salad. Serve chilled. Serves 6.

Lagniappe: This is a filling salad. Its carb count is almost too high, but it is a good salad to use when fruit is called for pairing with the main course. You can completely make this in advance and refrigerate until you are ready to serve. You can make a nice bed of lettuce to serve it on if you desire. Because this salad is sweet, it can also be used as a dessert.

Carbs per serving: 16.5 g.
Net carbs per serving: 14.5 g.
Calories per serving: 183

FRENCH SALAD DRESSING

¾ cup vegetable oil
¼ cup red wine vinegar
1 tsp. Tabasco® Sauce
1½ tsp. salt
1 tsp. white pepper, fresh ground

1 tsp. fresh basil, finely minced
½ tsp. fresh oregano, finely minced
2 tsp. Equal® sweetener
1 cup extra virgin olive oil

Add all the ingredients except for the olive oil to a blender or food processor and blend at full speed. Slowly drizzle in the olive oil while the blender or processor is on. The salad dressing should hold together well. Makes about 2 cups of salad dressing. Serving size is 2 tbsp.

Lagniappe: This dressing can and should be made in advance and refrigerated. The flavors have a better chance of blending together to give the dressing a full-bodied taste. Store any leftovers in the refrigerator for up to 1 week for full flavor. This is a great quick and easy salad dressing and is a real crowd-pleaser.

Carbs per serving: trace
Net Carbs per serving: trace
Calories per serving: 46

THOUSAND ISLAND SALAD DRESSING

2 cups real mayonnaise
4 hard boiled eggs, chopped
¼ cup dill pickle, finely chopped
2 tbsp. sweet pickle relish
2 tbsp. celery, chopped fine
½ cup low carb chili sauce (sugar free)

¼ cup of Worcestershire sauce
2 packets of Splenda® sweetener
1 tsp. garlic salt
1 tsp. Tabasco® Sauce
1 tsp. black pepper

Combine all the ingredients together and refrigerate for 1 hour before serving. Serve chilled. Serving size is 2 tbsp. Makes about 3 cups of dressing.

Lagniappe: This is a wonderful salad dressing. Just try it and you'll quit using the bought stuff and switch to this. It's easy to make and delicious. The dressing will keep for up to 5 days refrigerated.

Carbs per serving: 2.4 g.
Net carbs per serving: 2.2 g.
Calories per serving: 88

DIJON SALAD DRESSING

1 cup sour cream
¼ cup heavy whipping cream
2 tbsp. white wine vinegar
3 tbsp. Dijon mustard

1 tsp. fresh basil, minced fine
½ tsp. fresh parsley, minced fine
⅛ tsp. fresh dill, minced fine
⅛ tsp. fresh chives, minced fine

In a small mixing bowl, beat together the sour cream and the heavy whipping cream. Add the vinegar and the remaining ingredients and, using a wire whisk, beat together until the dressing is well blended. Cover and chill in the refrigerator for 2 hours. Makes about 1½ cup of dressing.

Lagniappe: This is such an easy, but delicious, salad dressing. You can store it in the refrigerator for up to two weeks if the sour cream you use is fresh. Be sure to check the expiration dates for the cream and sour cream before you start, you will generally have at least a 2 to 3 week window to use. This dressing is so good you'll want to have some left!

Carbs per tablespoon: 1 g.
Net Carbs per tablespoon: .9 g.
Calories per tablespoon: 39

CAESAR SALAD DRESSING

½ cup extra virgin olive oil
2 cloves garlic, minced
1 tsp. shallots, minced finely
¼ tbsp. red wine vinegar
1 tbsp. balsamic vinegar
3 tsp. Worcestershire sauce
⅓ cup Parmesan cheese, grated

1 tbsp. Romano cheese, grated
1 tsp. hot dry mustard
½ tsp. fresh basil, minced
1 tsp. salt
1 tsp. fresh ground black pepper
6 green olives with pimento

Combine all the ingredients in a blender or food processor and blend at high speed until the mixture is smooth. Store in a container that has a tight lid and use as you would any salad dressing. Makes about 1 cup of salad dressing. Serves 16.

Lagniappe: There is nothing better than fresh, homemade Caesar salad dressing. You can make this dressing up to 1 week in advance and use as needed. Any leftovers can be used for up to 1 week. It is best to use this within two days, but it is still good for up to a week. To change this dressing a little, you can add about 1 tbsp. of anchovy paste to the blender to give it an even richer taste. See note about balsamic vinegar on page 53.

Carbs per tbsp.: .7 g.
Net carbs per tbsp.: .6 g.
Calories per tbsp.: 73

SPINACH SALAD DRESSING EUPHEMIE

2 egg yolks, well beaten
⅓ cup white wine vinegar
1 tbsp. lemon juice, fresh
1 tsp. Grey Poupon® mustard
2 packets Splenda® sweetener
½ tsp. white pepper

1 tbsp. fresh chives, finely chopped
¼ tsp. garlic powder
½ tsp. salt
½ tsp. black pepper.
1 tsp. Tabasco® Sauce
2 cups extra virgin olive oil

Add all the ingredients into a food processor and blend at high speed. Gradually drizzle in the olive oil through the top until it is all blended into the dressing. Pour into a salad dressing bottle with a tight top and refrigerate until you are ready to use. Makes about 2½ cups of dressing.

Lagniappe: You can make this dressing in advance and store in the refrigerator for up to 3 days. It is a wonderful dressing for fresh spinach or for any salad for that matter. Be sure to keep the dressing refrigerated because the egg yolk is not cooked. The acid in the vinegar will keep it fresh, but do not leave it out from the refrigerator for long.

Carbs per tablespoon: trace
Net carbs per tablespoon: trace
Calories per tablespoon: 97

BLUE CHEESE SALAD DRESSING

1 cup mayonnaise
½ cup heavy whipping cream
½ cup blue cheese, crumbled
3 tbsp. onion, finely minced

1 tsp. Tabasco® Sauce
1 tsp. white Worcestershire sauce
½ tsp. salt

In a medium mixing bowl, add the mayonnaise and whipping cream; whip together with a wire whisk until well blended. Fold in the crumbled blue cheese. Add the remaining ingredients and blend well. Refrigerate for 2 hours and serve. Makes two cups of salad dressing.

Lagniappe: This may be made up to 1 week in advance and refrigerated until you are ready to use. This salad dressing that is low in carbs and high in taste. It is great as a dip for vegetables. I also like it with hot wings. Try it with sticks of fresh celery. What a taste!

Carbs per tbsp.: .3 g.
Net carbs per tbsp.: .3 g.
Calories per tbsp.: 30

FRESH AVOCADO SALAD DRESSING

½ cup vegetable oil
½ cup half-and-half cream
2 tbsp. heavy whipping cream
1 tbsp. balsamic vinegar
1 tsp. Tabasco® Sauce
1 tbsp. fresh lemon juice

1 tsp. salt
¼ tsp. fresh ground black pepper
1 packet Equal® sweetener
2 small avocado, peeled, seeded and well mashed

In a food processor with a metal blade, blend the oil on full power. Drizzle in the half-and-half and the heavy cream until mixed well. Leaving the blender on, drizzle in the vinegar, Tabasco, and lemon juice. Turn off the blender and add the remaining ingredients. Cover and turn the blender on full power for 1 minute or until all the avocado is blended into the dressing. Pour into a salad jar with a tight lid. Chill for 1 hour then serve. Makes about 2 cups of salad dressing.

Lagniappe: This dressing is great over green salad, tomato salad or cucumber salad. I also like it as a dip for fresh vegetables. It should keep its color because of the vinegar and lemon juice, as long as you store it in a tight jar in the refrigerator. This dressing will keep for 7 to 10 days. See note about balsamic vinegar on page 53.

Carbs per tbsp.: .8 g.
Net carbs per tbsp.: .6 g.
Calories per tbsp.: 44

Breakfast Dishes

EGG CUP BREAKFAST

2 tbsp. unsalted butter, softened

8 eggs

salt

fresh ground black pepper

¼ cup half-and-half

½ cup American cheese

½ cup Swiss cheese

Preheat the oven to 350 degrees. Grease 4 small soufflé or custard cups with the butter. Break two eggs into each cup; salt and pepper each to taste. Put 1 tbsp. cream on each egg and bake for 10 minutes. Egg should be barely set. Top each egg cup with an equal amount of both cheeses then return to the oven and bake for 2 more minutes. Serve hot right from the oven. Serves 4.

Lagniappe: This is simple and easy, but so good. It is a nice way to serve eggs to company. It looks special and tastes scrumptious. I usually serve it with sausage patties or links or with crisp bacon. This is a wonderful breakfast dish and it's nice on a breakfast buffet. Almost anything covered in cheese is delicious.

Carbs per serving: 1.9 g.
Net Carbs per serving: 1.9 g.
Calories per serving: 34

BAKED BREAKFAST EGGS

2 tbsp. unsalted butter
½ cup green onions, finely chopped
2 tbsp. red bell pepper, diced
1 tbsp. celery, minced
2 tbsp. whole wheat flour
1½ cup half-and-half
1 tsp. Tabasco® Sauce
½ tsp. salt

1 cup sharp cheddar cheese, grated
1 cup Swiss cheese, grated
½ cup American cheese, grated
8 hard boiled eggs, chopped
12 slices cooked bacon, crumbled
3 slices low-carb bread (5 carbs per slice), torn into small pieces

Preheat the oven to 350 degrees. Add the butter and let it melt and get hot. Add the onions, bell pepper, and celery and sauté for 5 minutes, stirring constantly. Add the flour and blend it in well, then add the cream slowly, stirring often until it starts to thicken, about 2 minutes. Add the cheeses and cook until they are melted and the sauce is nice and thick. Place half of the crumbled eggs in the bottom of a lightly-greased, 10 x 10 baking dish and pour half of the cheese sauce over the eggs. Sprinkle half of the torn bread on top, then repeat the process with the remaining eggs, cheese sauce, and bread. Bake uncovered for 18 minutes or until lightly browned. Let the dish stand for 5 minutes, then spoon out onto warm serving plates. Serve warm. Serves 6 to 8.

Lagniappe: This is a great breakfast dish. It's bacon, eggs, and cheese all together in a casserole. You can refrigerate the leftovers for later use. I like it cold right from the fridge. It can be completely put together and baked just before serving.

Carbs per serving: 1.9 g.
Net carbs per serving: 1.9 g.
Calories per serving: 342

BREAKFAST CASSEROLE

4 large eggs
1½ cup half-and-half
1 tsp. salt
1 tsp. fresh ground black pepper
1 tsp. Tabasco® Sauce
¼ cup red bell pepper, diced

1 10-oz. container frozen broccoli
  spears, thawed
8 slices of bacon, crumbled
½ cup American cheese, grated
½ cup Monterey Jack cheese, grated

Preheat the oven to 375 degrees. In a medium bowl, whip the eggs until well beaten with the salt, black pepper, and Tabasco® Sauce, then add the cream and mix in well. Pour into a lightly-greased 10 x 10 baking dish. Put the broccoli spears into the dish and spread out well. Sprinkle the bell pepper and bacon evenly around the dish, then evenly sprinkle both cheeses. Bake for 15 to 20 minutes or until the mixture is set. Cut into squares and serve. Serves 4.

Lagniappe: This is an easy and tasty breakfast dish. You can mix it together and refrigerate until you are ready to bake and serve. It makes ordinary eggs a little special. This is a nice side dish for meats, as well.

Carbs per serving: 1.9 g.
Net Carbs per serving: 1.9 g.
Calories per serving: 342

BREAKFAST EGG PIE

1 9-inch pie pan
butter for greasing the pan
3 eggs, well beaten
1 slice of low-carb bread, torn into pieces
1 cup half-and-half

1 tsp. salt
1 tsp. Tabasco® Sauce
¼ tsp. nutmeg
½ tsp. paprika
¼ tsp. fresh ground black pepper

Preheat the oven to 350 degrees. Lightly grease the pie pan with butter and set it aside for later use. In a medium mixing bowl, add the remaining ingredients and beat the egg mixture with a wire whisk until all the ingredients are mixed. Pour into the pie pan and bake for 25 minutes or until the pie is set and firm to the touch in the center of the pie. Remove and let the pie set for 1 minute, then cut it into four pieces and serve. Serves 4.

Lagniappe: This is another unusual way to have eggs in the morning. I like this because you can put the entire dish together in a mixing bowl (except for the eggs) the night before you plan to make it. When you are ready to bake, just beat the eggs well and add them to the cream/bread mixture, pour into the pie pan, and bake. It's really a quick and easy breakfast and a good way to start your morning. It's really a quiche without the pie shell. It serves as easy as quiche, but it doesn't have all the carbs in the pie crust!

Carbs per serving: 5.6 g.
Net carbs per serving: 3.8 g.
Calories per serving: 212

FRESH MUSHROOM CASSEROLE

1 low-carb tortillas (3 net carbs)
½ cup red bell pepper, diced
¼ cup green bell pepper, diced
¼ cup green onions, finely chopped
1 pound mushrooms, sliced
1 cup Monterey Jack cheese, grated
1 cup American cheese, grated
½ cup Swiss cheese, grated

1 cup cottage cheese
1 cup half-and-half
8 large eggs, slightly beaten
1 tsp. salt
1 tsp. fresh ground black pepper
1 tsp. Tabasco® Sauce
¼ cup fresh parsley, minced

Preheat the oven to 400 degrees. Lightly grease a 12 x 10 inch baking dish with unsalted butter. Chop the tortillas and sprinkle them on the bottom of the baking dish. Sprinkle the bell peppers and green onions on top of the tortillas, then evenly spread each of the cheeses on top of the tortillas and peppers. Evenly spread out the mushrooms over the entire dish. Put the cottage cheese in a food processor and blend until smooth. Add the half-and-half, eggs, salt, pepper, and Tabasco® Sauce and blend for 2 minutes. Pour over the cheese and sprinkle with the minced parsley. Bake for 30 minutes at 400 or until the dish is set. Serve hot. Serves 8.

Lagniappe: A filling breakfast treat or a wonderful mushroom side dish with meat, chicken, or seafood. You can completely assemble the dish and refrigerate for up to 24 hours before baking. This dish is wonderful either hot or cold. I like to eat a slice or two as a late-night snack right from the refrigerator. It is filling and curbs your late-night hunger. You can play around with other vegetables using the same recipe. Just add the fresh vegetable of your choice. When you add another vegetable, just take away some of the mushrooms so the recipe won't be too large for your baking pan. It's an excellent breakfast or snack.

Carbs per serving: 1.9 g.
Net Carbs per serving: 1.9 g.
Calories per serving: 342

OMELET LE CHAMPIGNON

1 tbsp. unsalted butter
½ cup mushrooms, sliced
⅛ cup green onions, chopped
⅛ cup bell pepper, finely diced
¼ cup fresh tomato, diced
1 tsp. fresh basil, minced

1 tsp. salt
1 tsp. fresh ground black pepper
1 tsp. Tabasco® Sauce
2 extra large eggs
1 tbsp. fresh parsley, minced

In a non-stick omelet pan over medium heat, heat the butter and melt. When the butter is melted and hot, add the mushrooms, green onions, bell pepper, tomatoes, and basil. Sauté for 3 minutes, stirring often. In a medium-sized mixing bowl, add the salt, black pepper, Tabasco® Sauce, and eggs. Beat the egg mixture until it begins to foam. Pour the egg mixture into the skillet and continue to cook. As the egg mixture begins to firm up, use a spatula to lift it from the side to the center, so the uncooked portion of the egg flows underneath When it is nearly all congealed, flip the omelet over and let it cook on the other side. When done, fold the omelet in half and sprinkle with the parsley. Serve hot. Serves one.

Lagniappe: This is the classic mushroom omelet. It is an easy and straightforward recipe. At times I like to add cheese. Just add the grated cheese of your choice when you are ready to fold the omelet in half. A great breakfast, brunch, lunch, or evening dish. Omelets are easy, a little showy, and, of course, very tasty. You can't go wrong with this one.

Carbs per serving: 1.9 g.
Net Carbs per serving: 1.9 g.
Calories per serving: 342

SALMON EGGS

4 large eggs
1 tbsp. half-and-half
1 tsp. salt
½ tsp. black pepper
2 tbsp. unsalted butter

6 oz. salmon, chopped
¼ cup sun dried tomatoes, chopped
1 tbsp. green onions, chopped
2 tbsp. Romano cheese, freshly grated
1 tbsp. fresh parsley, minced

In a medium-sized mixing bowl, beat the eggs well until they begin to foam. Add the half-and-half, salt and pepper. In a medium, heavy skillet melt the butter and let it get hot, then add the salmon, sun dried tomatoes, and green onions. Sauté for 3 minutes, stirring constantly. Pour the egg mixture into the skillet and cook uncovered for 2 minutes or until the mixture begins to set on the bottom. Using a spatula, lift and fold the partially uncooked eggs to the center, so that the uncooked portion flows underneath the cooked. Continue to cook for 2 more minutes. Sprinkle with the fresh grated cheese and parsley. Serve hot. Serves 2.

Lagniappe: This is a quick gourmet egg dish. Salmon is such a delicate fish and is appealing for breakfast, brunch, or even for dinner. Just spoon out a generous serving to your guest, leaving a generous portion for yourself. This is company food because of the look, name, and taste of the dish.

Carbs per serving: 1.9 g.
Net Carbs per serving: 1.9 g.
Calories per serving: 342

Seafood

SHRIMP SHERRY

2 lb. shrimp, peeled and deveined (21-25 shrimp)
2 tsp. Seafood Seasoning Mix (see p. 17)
1 stick unsalted butter, melted
½ cup of sherry wine

1 tbsp. Worcestershire sauce
1 tsp. Tabasco® Sauce
½ cup green onion tops, finely minced
¼ cup red bell pepper, minced
¼ cup parsley, finely minced

Preheat the oven to 425 degrees. Season the shrimp well with the Seafood Seasoning Mix and place in a shallow baking dish. Mix well together the butter, sherry, Worcestershire sauce, and Tabasco® Sauce and pour over the shrimp. Blend in the green onions and red pepper and sprinkle the dish with the parsley. Bake at 425 degrees for 20 minutes. Serve hot. Serves 6 as a main dish or 12 as an appetizer.

Lagniappe: This is quite an easy dish to make and there really is no reason to do anything in advance, but you can completely put the dish together ahead of time. Just sprinkle the parsley on top when you are ready to bake. Do not freeze the leftovers or prepare in advance and freeze. If you serve this as an appetizer you can plate individually or serve in a large dish on a buffet with. It is better to serve as an individual dish or appetizer because the bell pepper and green onions add so much flavor to the dish when eaten with the shrimp.

Carbs per 6 servings: 1.6 g.
Net Carbs 6 per servings: 1.2 g
Calories per 6 servings: 438

Carbs per 12 servings: .8 g
Net Carbs per 12 servings: .6 g
Calories per 12 servings: 219

SHRIMP MARIE

1 sticks unsalted butter
¼ cup bell pepper, diced
¼ cup onions, diced
3 cloves garlic, minced
2 green onion tops, minced
2 tbsp. celery, finely minced
3 tbsp. fresh lemon juice
2 tbsp. Worcestershire sauce

1 tsp. Tabasco® Sauce
2 lb. large shrimp (21-25's), peeled and deveined
½ cup of dry white wine
3 tbsp. fresh parsley, finely minced
1 Tsp. fresh ground black pepper
1 tsp. salt
1 tsp. Italian seasoning

Melt the butter in a large saucepan over medium heat. Preheat the oven to 375 degrees. In the saucepan with the butter, sauté the bell peppers, onion, garlic, green onions, and celery over medium heat until the vegetables are limp, about 5 minutes. Arrange the shrimp in 6 individual baking dishes and set aside. Add the remaining ingredients into the saucepan and bring to a boil, then reduce the heat and simmer over low heat for 5 minutes. Spoon equal amounts of the liquid butter mixture over the dishes equally. Place in the preheated oven and bake for 15 minutes at 375 degrees. The shrimp should be a nice pink color. Serve hot. Serves 8.

Lagniappe: This dish cannot be made in advance. However, you can always prepare the ingredients in advance and just mix them together as directed when you are ready to cook. This makes a great company dish, especially when you have guests that really like shrimp. You can always prepare this dish in one large casserole and allow everyone to serve the amount they wish from the one dish. It also makes a wonderful appetizer or buffet dish. If you serve it as an appetizer, just serve it with toothpicks on the side.

Carbs per serving: 2.9 g.
Net Carbs per serving: 2.5 g.
Calories per serving: 459

SHRIMP AND ARTICHOKE QUICHE

2 low-carb tortillas (3 carbs each)
½ cup Monterey Jack cheese, grated
½ cup Swiss cheese, grated
¼ cup sharp cheddar cheese, grated
1 cup boiled shrimp, peeled and
   deveined
1 cup artichoke hearts, chopped
½ cup onions, finely chopped

1 clove garlic, minced
¼ cup red bell pepper, diced finely
2 tbsp. celery, minced
1 tsp. Seafood Seasoning Mix (see
   p. 17)
1 tsp. Tabasco® Sauce
5 large eggs, beaten
1 cup half-and-half

Preheat the oven to 350 degrees. Cut the tortillas so they can be used to line the bottom of an non-stick 10-inch pie pan. Sprinkle each cheese evenly on top of the tortillas. Chop the shrimp a few times and spread them on top of the cheese. Arrange the artichoke hearts on top of the shrimp. Put all the remaining ingredients except for the egg and cream into a small mixing bowl and stir together. Beat the egg and cream together well, then pour into the mixing bowl with the seasonings. Stir together well, then pour it into the pie pan with the shrimp and artichoke. Bake at 350 for about 35 minutes or until firmly set. Check with a toothpick in the center of the quiche; if it comes out clean then the pie is ready. If not, continue to cook for 5 more minutes. Remove from the oven and let the quiche sit for 3 minutes then cut into pieces. Serve warm. Serves 6.

Lagniappe: Quiche is a nice company meal and it's great for a buffet or brunch. I happen to think it's great breakfast fare, but many think this is a noon or dinner dish. Whenever you like to eat it, you will love this easy quiche recipe. Basically you just throw it together and bake. You can also make Lump Crabmeat and Artichoke Quiche using this same recipe. Just substitute ½ pound of lump crabmeat for the shrimp and follow the recipe as above.

Carbs per serving: 10.9 g.
Net carbs per serving: 4.9 g.
Calories per serving: 275

BROILED SHRIMP CAYENNE

1 clove garlic, minced
1 tsp. Cayenne pepper
1 tsp. paprika
1 tsp. salt
½ tsp. black pepper

1 tsp. Tabasco® Sauce
2 tbsp. extra virgin olive oil
1 tbsp. fresh lemon juice
2 pounds shrimp (15-20's), peeled and
    deveined

Preheat the oven to broil. Mix together the garlic, cayenne, paprika, salt, black pepper, Tabasco® Sauce, olive oil, and lemon juice in a medium mixing bowl with a wire whist to form a marinade. Coat the shrimp well by dipping each shrimp tail into the marinade. Set aside in a large glass bowl until you are ready to broil. Place the shrimp on a flat broiling pan and broil for 3 minutes on each side. Serve hot immediately from the oven. Serves six.

Lagniappe: You can use the same recipe and grill the shrimp on an indoor or outdoor grill. Just make sure the grill is hot and follow the same procedure as broiling. This is a wonderful appetizer or main dish. I serve it with a salad with lots of different greens, tomatoes, cucumbers, and whatever is in season. You can add these broiled shrimp to a salad for a wonderful broiled shrimp salad. Another suggestion is to make shrimp salad with these broiled shrimp for a nice change.

Carbs per serving: .5 g.
Net carbs per serving: .4 g.
Calories per serving: 193

LOW-CARB SHRIMP AU GRATIN

¼ stick butter

1 pound mushrooms, cleaned and sliced

6 green onions, finely chopped

½ red bell pepper, diced

1 tbsp. celery, minced

2 tsp. flour, all purpose

2 pounds boiled shrimp, peeled and deveined

¾ cup heavy whipping cream

1 pound Monterey Jack cheese, cut into cubes

½ pound sharp cheddar cheese, cut into cubes

½ pound Gruyère cheese, cut into cubes

¼ cup fresh parsley, finely minced

1 slice of low-carb bread (5 carbs), buttered and toasted in the oven at low temperature until quite dry then put into a food processor to be made into breadcrumbs

Preheat the oven to 350 degrees. In a large saucepan over medium heat, melt the butter, then add the mushrooms, onions, bell pepper, and celery; sauté for 5 minutes or until the vegetables are limp. Add the flour and blend in well and cook for 3 more minutes, stirring constantly. Add the heavy cream and blend in well. Add the cheeses and stir until they are melted, about 5 minutes. Pour into lightly-greased individual au gratin dishes, sprinkle with parsley and 1 tablespoon of homemade bread crumbs (made from low-carb bread) each. Bake at 350 degrees for 12 minutes and serve right from the oven. Serves 6.

Lagniappe: This is a wonderful low-carb au gratin. It is easy to do and can be made in advance and refrigerated until ready to serve. Or it can be frozen for later use. If you freeze it, completely thaw, then bake for the 12 minutes as above and serve. This au gratin can be made with lump crabmeat to make Low-Carb Lump Crabmeat au Gratin. Just use fresh lump crabmeat right from the container or you can use fresh sea scallops to make Low-Carb Scallops au Gratin. No matter how you make it, it's wonderful!

Carbs per serving: 18.6 g.
Net carbs per serving: 14.6 g.
Calories per serving: 868

BAKED EGGPLANT WITH SHRIMP

2 medium eggplants, cut into large
   cubes
cold water to cover the eggplant
2 tsp. salt
1 tsp. Tabasco® Sauce
½ stick unsalted butter
2 medium yellow onions, chopped
1 large bell pepper, chopped

¼ cup of celery, minced
3 cloves of garlic, minced
2 pounds shrimp, (21-25's), peeled
   and deveined
2 tsp. Seafood Seasoning Mix (see
   p. 17 for recipe)
2 slices of low-carb bread (5 carbs per
   slice)

Preheat the oven to 375 degrees. Put the eggplant into a large pot that has a strainer, cover with cold water, add the salt and Tabasco® Sauce, and bring to a boil. Reduce to a low, rolling boil and let it cook for 5 minutes. Remove from the heat and drain the eggplant well until almost all of the water is drained. In a large saucepan over medium-high heat, add the butter and let it melt and get hot. Add the onions, bell pepper, celery, and garlic. Sauté for 6 minutes, then add the eggplant and continue to cook, stirring often, for 3 more minutes. Add the shrimp and Seafood Seasoning Mix. Cook for 5 more minutes. Then tear the two slices of bread into small pieces and mix into the shrimp/eggplant mixture. Pour into 6 individual serving dishes or one large casserole dish and bake for 25 minutes. Serve immediately. Serves 6.

Lagniappe: This is a wonderful dish for those who like either shrimp or eggplant! It can be a main dish or it can be used as a side dish. If you use it as a side dish it will serve 10. You can use this same recipe and add lump crabmeat instead of the shrimp to make Baked Eggplant with Lump Crabmeat. You just substitute the crabmeat for the shrimp and cook as above, except you do not cook the crabmeat in the skillet before you mix together to bake. Mix the crabmeat with the eggplant, blend together well and pour into the baking dish or dishes and bake. You can also use this same recipe to make Baked Eggplant with Oysters by following the recipe above, but substituting oysters for the crabmeat. Just blend the oysters into the cooked eggplant mixture, add the torn bread, and bake as usual. These are great alternative dishes.

Carbs per serving: 19.3 g.
Net carbs per serving: 12.4 g.
Calories per serving: 281

SHRIMP REMOULADE

¼ cup Creole mustard
2 tbsp. red wine vinegar
1 tbsp. prepared horseradish
2 tbsp. paprika
1 tsp. Tabasco® Sauce
1 tsp. fresh ground black pepper
1 tsp. salt
½ tsp. cayenne pepper
¼ cup extra virgin olive oil

½ cup green onion, finely minced
3 cloves garlic, minced
2 tbsp. celery, finely minced
2 tbsp. bell pepper, finely minced
2 tbsp. fresh parsley, finely minced
2 pounds shrimp, boiled, peeled and deveined
1 head lettuce, shredded

In a large mixing bowl, blend together the Creole mustard, vinegar, horseradish, paprika, Tabasco® Sauce, black pepper, salt, and cayenne pepper until well mixed. Slowly drizzle the olive oil into the mixture and using a wire whisk, blend together the mustard mixture and the olive oil until all the oil is used. Fold in the remaining ingredients except for the shrimp and lettuce and mix together well. Add the shrimp to the sauce mixture and completely coat the shrimp with the sauce. Cover tightly and refrigerate overnight. When you are ready to serve, place a generous portion of the shredded lettuce on a salad or dinner plate and spoon a generous portion of shrimp and the Remoulade sauce onto the lettuce. Serve chilled. Serves 8.

Lagniappe: This is a shrimp salad to die for! This sauce is wonderful with shrimp, but it also can be used as a marinade for cracked crab claws. To make Crab Claws Remoulade, just make the dish as above, but add the crab claws to the sauce and refrigerate overnight and serve on top of shredded lettuce. No matter how you serve Remoulade it is delicious. You can make the dish up to 48 hours in advance and store tightly covered in the refrigerator until you are ready to serve. This is an excellent party dish or covered dish treat.

Carbs per serving: 4.1 g.
Net carbs per serving: 2.6 g.
Calories per serving: 193

SHRIMP IMPERIAL

3 tbsp. unsalted butter
½ cup onions, chopped
½ cup bell pepper, chopped
2 tbsp. celery, minced
1 clove garlic, minced
1½ pound of shrimp, peeled and
   deveined
3 tbsp. soy flour
1 tsp. dry hot mustard

1 cup half-and-half
2 tbsp. lemon juice
1 tsp. Worcestershire sauce
1 tsp. Seafood Seasoning Mix (see p. 17)
1 tsp. Tabasco® Sauce
¼ cup pimento, drained and diced
¼ cup mayonnaise
butter for greasing the baking dishes
paprika for dusting top

In a large heavy skillet over medium-high heat, add the butter and let it melt and get hot. When hot, add the onions, bell pepper, celery, and garlic. Sauté for 2 minutes, stirring constantly. Add the shrimp and sauté for 5 more minutes, stirring constantly. Reduce the heat to low, add the flour and blend in well, and cook for 2 minutes, stirring constantly. In a mixing bowl, combine all the other ingredients except for the butter for greasing and the paprika and beat well together with a wire whisk, whipping until the mixture is smooth. Pour into the skillet and blend together well. Pour into individual baking dishes or one large baking dish, dust with the paprika, and bake for 15 minutes at 350 degrees. Serve hot. Serves 4.

Lagniappe: This dish can be completely made and refrigerated before baking. Just bake as above right from the refrigerator when you are ready to cook. You can use this same recipe to make Lump Crabmeat Imperial by substituting 1 pound of lump crabmeat for the shrimp. Add the crabmeat to the dish by folding it into the bowl with the beaten mayonnaise/pimento mixture. Then just pour and bake as above. You can also make Scallops Imperial by substituting 1½ pounds of sea scallops for the shrimp above and cooking the same way you would shrimp. Finally, you can make wonderful Crawfish Imperial by substituting 1½ pounds of crawfish for the shrimp and cooking as you would the shrimp or scallops. No matter how you fix it, you'll love the outcome. Enjoy!

Carbs per serving: 7.7 g.
Net carbs per serving: 5.8 g.
Calories per serving: 448

SHRIMP LEBLANC

2 sticks unsalted butter
¼ cup bell peppers, chopped
¼ cup onions, chopped
3 cloves garlic, minced
¼ cup green onion tops, minced
1 tbsp. celery, minced
3 tbsp. lemon juice
3 tbsp. Worcestershire sauce

2 tsp. Tabasco® Sauce
2 lbs. large shrimp, peeled and
  deveined
⅔ cup dry white wine
¼ cup parsley, minced
1 tsp. fresh ground black pepper
1¾ tsp. salt
1 tsp. Italian seasoning

Melt the butter in a large skillet over medium heat. Preheat the oven to 375 degrees. In the skillet, sauté the bell pepper, onion, garlic, green onion, and celery until limp, about 5 minutes. Arrange the shrimp in 8 individual baking dishes and spoon equal amounts of the butter sauce over them. Combine the remaining ingredients in another saucepan over medium heat. Bring the wine mixture to a boil then reduce the heat to low and simmer for 5 Minutes. Meanwhile, place the baking dishes in the oven and bake at 375 degrees for 10 minutes. Remove the dishes from the oven and spoon equal amounts of the wine sauce into each dish. Stir the wine through and place the dishes back in the oven for another 7 minutes. The shrimp should be a nice pink color. Serve hot. Serves 8.

Lagniappe: This dish cannot be made in advance. However, you can prepare all the ingredients in advance and just mix them together as directed. This excellent dish makes a nice company meal, especially for guests who really like shrimp. You can do the same dish with lump crabmeat to make Lump Crabmeat LeBlanc. Just use 1 pound lump crabmeat instead of shrimp and follow the direction as above.

Carbs per serving: 3.2 g.
Net carbs per serving: 2.8 g.
Calories per serving: 339

SHRIMP BONIN

1 lb. large shrimp (21-25's)
1 tsp. Seafood Seasoning Mix (see p. 17)
1 medium onion, sliced and separated into rings

2 cloves garlic, minced
1 stick unsalted butter
1 tbsp. extra virgin olive oil
½ cup brandy

Peel and devein the shrimp, leaving the tip of the tail on each. Butterfly the shrimp by splitting each along the back almost completely through and spreading the halves apart into a butterfly shape. Season the shrimp evenly with the Seafood Seasoning Mix. Combine the shrimp, onion rings, and garlic well in a mixing bowl. Cover the bowl tightly with plastic wrap and let it refrigerate for at least two hours.

In a large heavy skillet over medium-high heat, melt the butter, then add the olive oil. When the butter starts to turn light brown, add the shrimp, onions, and garlic. Sauté for 5 minutes, shaking the pan gently to keep the shrimp from sticking. Reduce the heat to low and carefully add the brandy. Strike a match away from the pan then tilt the pan a little and light the brandy. Be careful at this stage; there will be a "puff" as the brandy lights. Let the dish burn until it burns itself out. Serve immediately. Serves 4 as a main dish or 8 as an appetizer.

Lagniappe: All you can do in advance is peel and devein the shrimp, cut the onions, and mince the garlic, then set them aside in the refrigerator as per the recipe. You can let them set for up to 24 hours if you wish. This will save you some time when you are ready to cook. This is a quick and showy dish that is excellent for company because there will be no doubt that you cooked the dish!

For 4 servings:
Carbs per serving: 5.7 g.
Net carbs per serving: 4.6 g.
Calories per serving: 436

For 8 servings:
Carbs per serving: 2.8 g.
Net carbs per serving: 2.3 g.
Calories per serving: 218

SHRIMP ASHLEY

2 tbsp. unsalted butter
1 cup green onions, minced
3 cloves garlic, minced
1 tbsp. celery, minced
2 pounds shrimp, peeled and deveined
1½ tsp. Seafood Seasoning Mix (see
   p. 17)

1 tbsp. soy flour
1 tsp. Worcestershire sauce
1 tsp. Tabasco® Sauce
1 tsp. sweet basil, minced
2 cups sour cream

In a large, heavy skillet over medium-high heat, melt the butter and let it get hot. Add the onions, garlic, and celery and sauté for 3 minutes. Add the shrimp and Seafood Seasoning Mix and sauté for 5 more minutes, stirring constantly. Add the soy flour and sauté for 2 minutes, stirring constantly. Add the Worcestershire, Tabasco® Sauce, and sweet basil and blend in well. Reduce the heat to low and gradually add in the sour cream a little at a time. Heat until well mixed. Do not boil. Serve immediately. Serves 6.

Lagniappe: This is a great and simple dish. It is quite easy but the taste is fantastic. I like to serve it in a bowl with lots of the liquid from the skillet. Do not make in advance. You can refrigerate after cooking, but do not freeze. The dish is best eaten right after initial cooking.

Carbs per serving: 5.5 g.
Net Carbs per serving: 4.8 g.
Calories per serving: 360

SHRIMP SCAMPI

2 lb. shrimp, peeled and deveined
2 tsp. Seafood Seasoning Mix (see
  p. 17)
4 cloves garlic, finely minced
⅓ cup extra virgin olive oil

½ cup extra dry vermouth
1 tsp. black pepper, coarsely ground
3 tbsp. lemon juice
¼ cup fresh parsley, minced

In a large heavy skillet over medium-high heat, add the olive oil and let it get hot. Add the shrimp, Seafood Seasoning Mix, and garlic and sauté for 7 minutes. When the shrimp are cooked, add the vermouth and black pepper; continue to cook until the liquid is almost gone. Add the lemon juice and stir in well, then sprinkle with the parsley and serve immediately. Serves 6.

Lagniappe: This is shrimp at its best—sautéed and served hot. This is a quick and simple dish that really highlights the taste of the shrimp. You can't do anything in advance. You should also plan on eating all the dish and not saving leftovers. This is a dish that is outstanding, but only right after being cooked.

Carbs per serving: 1.6 g.
Net carbs per serving: 1.4 g.
Calories per serving: 276

SHRIMP CHETANIER

1 stick unsalted butter
6 green onions, chopped
½ pound mushrooms, sliced
3 cloves garlic, finely minced
½ cup red bell pepper, finely diced
2 tbsp. fresh basil, finely chopped
3 pounds uncooked shrimp, peeled and deveined

1½ tsp. salt
1½ tsp. fresh ground black pepper
1 tsp. Tabasco® Sauce
¼ cup dry white wine
1 cup sour cream
1 tsp. ThickenThin Not/Starch® thickener

In a large saucepan over medium-high heat, add the butter and let it melt and start to sizzle. Sauté the green onions, mushrooms, garlic, red pepper, and sweet basil for 4 minutes. Add the shrimp, salt, and black pepper and sauté for 6 minutes, stirring often. Remove the pan from the heat and add the Tabasco® Sauce, white wine, sour cream, and thickener; stir until well blended, then return to the heat. Cook, stirring constantly, until the sauce is light, creamy, and coats the spoon well, about 3 minutes. Serve hot. Serves 6.

Lagniappe: What an easy and wonderfully delicious dish. The sauce that the wine and sour cream makes is out of this world. I do not recommend making this dish in advance because it is so quick and the sauce has a much better texture when eaten right after making. Serve with a vegetable and a green salad and you've got an exciting meal.

Carbs per serving: 7.2 g.
Net carbs per serving: 5.5 g.
Calories per serving: 474

OYSTERS SIDONIA

4 dozen large oysters
16 strips of bacon, cut into thirds
toothpicks
½ cup dry red wine
2 tsp. Tabasco® Sauce

1 tbsp. Worcestershire sauce
1 tbsp. fresh lemon juice
3 cloves garlic, minced
1 tsp. onion powder
2 tsp. Seafood Seasoning Mix (see p. 17)

Wrap each oyster with ⅓ of a strip of bacon and fasten the bacon with a toothpick. Mix the wine, Tabasco®, Worcestershire, lemon juice, and onion powder in a deep bowl until well blended. Add the bacon-wrapped oysters. Refrigerate for 3 hours. Preheat the oven to 475 degrees. Remove the oysters from the refrigerator and evenly season them with the Seafood Seasoning Mix. Bake at 475 degrees for 5 minutes, then baste well with the marinating liquid. Turn the oysters and bake for 5 more minutes at 475. Baste once more, then reduce the heat to 350 degrees and bake for 5 more minutes. Serve hot. Serves 4 as a main course or 8 as an appetizer.

Lagniappe: You can marinate the oysters for up to 36 hours in advance before baking, if you like. Do not cook in advance and refrigerate or freeze this dish. Serve the oysters right from the oven. This is as good as fried oysters, since the bacon does fry the oysters while it is cooking. You get both baked and fried oysters.

As a Main Course:
Carbs per serving: 11.5 g.
Net carbs per serving 11.3 g.
Calories per serving: 330

As an Appetizer:
Carbs per serving: 5.7 g.
Net carbs per serving: 5.7 g.
Calories per serving: 165

SAUTÉED OYSTERS

1 stick unsalted butter
⅓ cup low-carb beer
3 cups oysters
5 cloves garlic, minced
1 tsp. salt

1 tsp. black pepper
1 tsp. Tabasco® Sauce
½ tsp. cayenne pepper
1 cup green onions, chopped
2 cups fresh mushrooms, sliced

Combine the first three ingredients together in a large heavy skillet over medium-high heat. Cook for 5 minutes, stirring occasionally. Remove the oysters from the skillet and set them aside in a bowl. Add the remaining ingredients to the skillet and cook until most of the liquid is gone, about 15 minutes, then return the oysters to the skillet and continue to cook until most of the remaining juice is gone. Serve hot. Serves 4.

Lagniappe: This is the dish for oyster lovers! The oysters are tender and the remaining liquid is so full of flavor you will want to lick the pan. The oysters and the mushrooms together make a delightful treat. If you are pressed for time, you can do the first part of the recipe in advance and refrigerate until you are ready to serve. Then return the oysters to the skillet for the final cooking over medium heat, about 5 to 7 minutes.

Carbs per serving: 13.6 g.
Net carbs per serving: 9.6 g.
Calories per serving: 360

SEARED SEA SCALLOPS WITH GREEN ONION CREAM

1 cup heavy whipping cream
¼ cup green onion tops, thinly chopped
1 tsp. Tabasco® Sauce
1½ tsp. Splenda® sweetener
2 tsp. red bell pepper, finely diced
24 fresh sea scallops, about 1 inch each

2 tsp. Seafood Seasoning Mix (see p. 17)
¼ cup extra virgin olive oil
2 tbsp. shallots, finely minced
3 cloves garlic, finely minced
½ cup fresh parsley, finely minced

In a medium-sized, glass mixing bowl, add the cream, green onion tops, Tabasco® Sauce, and Splenda® and whip at high speed until moderate peaks begin to form. Fold the red bell peppers into the whipped cream, taking care not to break the peaks too much. Cover the bowl with plastic wrap and place in the refrigerator for later use. Season the scallops evenly with the Seafood Seasoning Mix. In a large, heavy saucepan over medium-high heat, add the olive oil and heat until the oil starts to pop. Add the shallots and garlic and sauté for 3 minutes, then add the scallops, taking care to only brown each side evenly. You should be able to cook 12 at a time. When the first 12 have browned nicely on both sides, about 3 minutes on each side, remove to a warm plate and repeat the process until all scallops are browned. Put the scallops back into the skillet and heat for 1 minute, then arrange 6 large scallops on each of four serving plates. Cover generously with the green onion whip, sprinkle with fresh parsley, and serve immediately. Serves 4.

Lagniappe: Don't let the length of this recipe scare you. It is simple and easy to make. Sea scallops are such a good seafood to cook with and you will love the whip on top. It is a dish that you will remember for a long time. It is beautiful and you will find yourself wanting to lick the plate. You can use the same recipe to make Seared Prawns with Green Onion Cream by substituting 32 extra-large shrimp for the scallops. Either way, you are in for a treat!

For Scallops:
Carbs per serving: 9.5 g.
Net Carbs per serving: 8.9 g.
Calories per serving: 565

For Shrimp:
Carbs per serving: 3.4 g.
Net carbs per serving: 2.9 g.
Calories per serving: 563

SEARED SCALLOPS ERATH

24 fresh sea scallops, washed in cold water and patted dry
2 tsp. Seafood Seasoning Mix (see p. 17)
½ tsp. fresh oregano, chopped
½ tsp. fresh basil, finely chopped
¼ cup extra virgin olive oil

3 cloves garlic, finely minced
¼ cup green onion bottoms, finely chopped
½ cup dry sherry wine
1 tbsp. balsamic vinegar
½ cup fresh parsley, minced

Season the scallops with the Seafood Seasoning Mix, fresh oregano, and basil. In a medium, heavy skillet over medium-high heat, add the olive oil and heat until it begins to pop. Add the scallops and cook for 3 minutes on each side. You can cook about half the scallops at a time. Remove when finished to a warm plate and repeat the process until all are cooked. Add the garlic and onion bottoms and sauté for 4 minutes, then add the wine and vinegar. Cook, reducing the wine for 2 minutes, constantly stirring. Add the scallops and sauté in the liquid for 3 more minutes. Sprinkle in the fresh parsley and serve hot. Serves 4.

Lagniappe: This is quick and easy, yet quite excellent. Do not make in advance as the scallops' texture tends to lessen when stored in the refrigerator. The scallops should be crisp on the outside and very tender and juicy inside. Serve with a crisp green salad. See note about balsamic vinegar on page 53.

Carbs per serving: 8.3 g.
Net carbs per serving: 7.9 g.
Calories per serving: 285

CRAWFISH FLAMBÉ ABBEVILLE

1 cup of Seafood Stock (see p. 89)

2 tbsp. unsalted butter

2 shallots, finely minced

1 carrot, finely diced

1 small tomato, peeled, seeded, and finely chopped

1 tbsp. red bell pepper, minced

2 cloves garlic, finely minced

1 tbsp. celery, minced

1 bay leaf

1 tbsp. fresh parsley, minced

1 tsp. Seafood Seasoning Mix (see p. 17)

1 tsp. paprika

½ stick unsalted butter

2 pounds crawfish, peeled and deveined

½ tsp. cayenne pepper

6 green onions, chopped

¼ cup of brandy

1½ cup heavy whipping cream

1 tbsp brandy

Bring the Seafood Stock to a boil, then reduce the heat to a very low simmer. In a large saucepan over medium-high heat, add the two tablespoons of butter and let it melt and start to smoke. Add the shallots, carrot, tomato, bell pepper, garlic, celery, bay leaf, and parsley and sauté for 4 minutes, stirring constantly. Season the crawfish with the Seafood Seasoning Mix and paprika. Put the additional ½ cup of butter into the pan and, when it is melted and begins to sizzle, add the crawfish, cayenne, and green onions and stir in well. When the crawfish are hot, add the brandy and carefully flambé. Be sure that the skillet is stable and that you just lightly shake the pan, to be sure that the brandy does not spill. Flambé until the flame goes out. Add the warm Seafood Stock and let it come to a boil, then reduce the heat to a simmer. Add the heavy whipping cream and the remaining tablespoon of brandy. Blend together well. Serve hot. Serves 8.

Lagniappe: This recipe has a lot of ingredients and calls for a flambé, but don't let it scare you. My grandma used to say, "Cher, make dem tink that you don't know all de tings you got in de pot!" Translation: "Baby, don't let them know all the good things you put into the dish! You don't want it to be too easy for them to figure out what you've done!" Ah, the life of a great Cajun cook! It's full of secrets—secrets that I'm sharing with you now.

Carbs per serving: 6.9 g.
Net carbs per serving: 6.2 g.
Calories per serving: 429

CRABMEAT LEMOINE

1 lb. lump crabmeat

1½ tsp. Seafood Seasoning Mix (see p. 17)

1½ cup fresh mushrooms, sliced

6 tsp. unsalted butter

¾ cup Gouda cheese, grated

¾ cup American cheese, grated

Preheat the oven to 400 degrees. Put equal amounts of crabmeat into each of 6 individual ramekins. Season equally with the Seafood Seasoning Mix. Place equal amounts of mushrooms on top of the crabmeat and dot with the tsp. of butter. Sprinkle the two cheeses evenly and lightly dust with paprika. Bake for 10 minutes at 400 degrees. The cheese should be melted and lightly browned. Serve immediately. Serves 6.

Lagniappe. This dish is awesome. Serve it as the main dish or serve it with a filet mignon to have a surf and turf. Lump crabmeat is so delicious and delicate that you would really have to try to mess up any dish with it. You don't have to kill yourself to serve great food. You can set this dish all up and refrigerate. Pull out of the refrigerator about 10 minutes before you are ready to serve. This dish will make you say with a big smile, "This is a h—l of a diet!"

Carbs per serving: 2.1 g.

Net carbs per serving: 1.8 g.

Calories per serving: 262

SAUTÉED LUMP CRABMEAT

½ stick unsalted butter
3 cloves garlic, finely minced
1 shallot, finely minced
2 tbsp. celery, finely minced
2 tbsp. red bell pepper, diced

1 pound fresh lump crabmeat
1 tsp. Seafood Seasoning Mix (see p. 17)
1 tsp. Tabasco® Sauce
¼ tbsp. fresh parsley, finely minced

Melt the butter in a medium saucepan over medium heat until hot. Add the garlic, shallot, celery, and bell pepper and sauté for 4 minutes, stirring often. Add the crabmeat, Seafood Seasoning Mix, and Tabasco® Sauce and gently sauté for 3 more minutes. Sprinkle with the fresh minced parsley. Serve hot. Serves 6.

Lagniappe: This is a meal in itself or it can be used as a topping for seafood or meats. Crabmeat is so delicate and delicious. Your imagination is the only limit. Crabmeat enhances other dishes and it's wonderful by itself. It can be served hot, warm, or cold.

Carbs per serving: 1.5 g.
Net carbs per serving: 1.2 g.
Calories per serving: 150

LUMP CRABMEAT AU GRATIN

1 stick unsalted butter
1 large onion, minced
½ cup celery, minced
2 cloves garlic, minced
¼ cup red bell pepper, diced
¼ cup soy flour
1¼ cup heavy whipping cream
4 large egg yolks, beaten
1 tsp. salt
1 tsp. Tabasco® Sauce

½ tsp. white pepper
½ tsp. black pepper
1 lb. lump crabmeat
1 cup Swiss cheese, grated
2 tbsp. pimento, diced
2 tbsp. fresh parsley, minced
¼ cup green onions, minced
1 cup American cheese, grated
1 cup sharp cheddar cheese, grated
butter to grease baking dish or dishes

Preheat the oven to 375 degrees. In a large skillet over medium heat, add the butter and melt. When the butter is hot, add the onion, celery, garlic, and red bell pepper; sauté for 5 minutes, stirring constantly. Add the soy flour and cook for 2 minutes, stirring often. Then gently add the cream and stir until all the flour is absorbed. Take some of the liquid and put it into the beaten egg in a small metal bowl to slowly increase the temperature of the egg. Once you have about 1 cup of egg/cream mixture in the bowl, pour it into the skillet. Add the salt, Tabasco® Sauce, and white and black pepper to the skillet and blend in well. Reduce the heat to low and cook the sauce for 4 minutes, stirring constantly. Put in the crabmeat, taking care not to break the nice lumps. Add the Swiss cheese, pimento, parsley, and green onions and carefully stir them into the mixture. Mix together the American and cheddar cheese and set aside. Lightly grease with butter either individual au gratin dishes or a large au gratin dish and pour the crabmeat mixture into each container. Cover well with the grated cheese and bake for 15 minutes at 375 degrees or until the casserole is golden brown. Serve hot. Serves 6.

Lagniappe: You can make this dish completely in advance and refrigerate up to 3 days before baking. You can also freeze this dish either before baking or after baking. To freeze it after baking, be sure to cover the dish tightly with plastic wrap. To reheat, thaw in the refrigerator until defrosted, then bake at 300 for 12 to 15 minutes. To freeze before baking, cover it tightly and freeze. When you are ready to bake, thaw in the refrigerator and bake for 17 minutes at 375 degrees. You can also use this same recipe to make Crawfish au Gratin. Just substitute 1½ pounds of crawfish for the pound of crabmeat and proceed as above. You can also make Shrimp au Gratin by substituting 1½ pounds of peeled and deveined shrimp for the crabmeat. Cook as above, except add the shrimp when you sauté the onion, celery, garlic, and bell pepper and sauté for 7 minutes instead of 5. Finally, you can make wonderful Scallops au Gratin by substituting 1½ pounds scallops for the shrimp and cooking as you would the shrimp. Any way you serve it, au Gratin is a hit!

Carbs per serving: 8.6 g.
Net carbs per serving: 6.5 g.
Calories per serving: 560

LUMP CRABMEAT VERMOUTH

3 cups heavy whipping cream
½ cup of dry vermouth
1 tsp. Seafood Seasoning Mix (see
    p. 17)

½ tsp. white pepper, freshly ground
1 pound fresh lump crabmeat

Place the cream into a medium saucepan and turn heat to a simmer. Pour in vermouth and place over low heat and reduce the liquid to about ½ the amount, stirring often. Add the remaining ingredients and fold crabmeat into the sauce. Pour into 8 individual au gratin or single ceramic shells. Bake at 350 degrees for 25 minutes and serve. Serves 8.

Lagniappe: This is a perfect appetizer or it can be a main dish by increasing the amount served and reducing the serving size to 6. This is an easy, yet elegant recipe. You can make in advance and refrigerate. Either completely cook and then refrigerate or you can hold before cooking, then cook for 5 extra minutes. If you completely cook, you will only need to heat the dish for about 12 minutes before serving.

Carbs per serving: 2.6 g.
Net carbs per serving: 2.6 g.
Calories per serving: 381

CATFISH DESIRE

6 catfish filets, about 6 oz. each
1 tsp. Seafood Seasoning Mix (see
   p. 17)
1 tbsp. unsalted butter
¼ cup onions, finely chopped
1 clove garlic, minced

½ cup celery, finely chopped
1 tsp. whole wheat flour
1 cup heavy whipping cream
1 tsp. Tabasco® Sauce
¾ cup cheddar cheese, grated
1 tsp. Paprika

Preheat the oven to 400 degrees. Wash the fish in cold water, then pat dry with paper towels and season with the seasoning mix. Set aside for later use. In a medium skillet over medium heat, melt the butter and let it get hot. Add the onion, garlic and celery and sauté for 5 minutes, stirring often. Add the flour and stir into the mixture and let it cook for 3 minutes, stirring constantly. Remove from the heat and add the cream and Tabasco® Sauce. Return to the heat and cook over low heat for 6 minutes, stirring constantly. Place the fish in a baking dish and cover with the cream sauce. Top the fish with the cheese and dust with the paprika. Bake for 20 minutes. Serve hot. Serves 6.

Lagniappe: Catfish is an easy fish to cook and it always comes out great. If your filets are frozen, make sure they are completely thawed before using. Catfish does freeze well; just take care not to tear the fish when defrosting. Let it thaw in the refrigerator. Don't try to rush things by defrosting in the microwave, as the fish is so tender it will begin to cook before you try to bake it and it will significantly lose flavor and texture.

Carbs per serving: 2.9 g.
Net carbs per serving: 2.6 g.
Calories per serving: 457

BROILED CATFISH

8 catfish filets, bout 6 oz. each
1 cup unsalted butter and melted
2 tsp. Seafood Seasoning Mix (see
    p. 17 for recipe)

1 tsp. paprika
¼ cup fresh parsley, minced
3 tbsp. fresh lemon juice

Preheat the oven to 400 degrees. Place the catfish in an ovenproof pan and pour melted butter over it. Be sure the bottom of the pan is covered with butter. Sprinkle each filet evenly with Seafood Seasoning Mix, paprika, and fresh parsley. Bake at 400 degrees until the fish is done, about 20 minutes. When you remove the fish from the oven, sprinkle them liberally with the lemon juice and serve immediately. Serves 8.

Lagniappe: This is quick and easy, but so good. Catfish is a natural crowd pleaser. The flesh is tender and sweet and the lemon juice sets it up nicely. You can set this recipe up in advance and get it ready to bake. When you are ready, just pop it into the oven and bake.

Carbs per serving: 1.4 g.
Net carbs per serving: 1.2 g.
Calories per serving: 599

CAJUN CATFISH

2 tsp. Seafood Seasoning Mix (see
   p. 17)
6 farm-raised catfish filets, 6 oz. each
¼ cup unsalted butter

    Season each catfish filet equally with the Seafood Seasoning Mix. In a heavy skillet over high heat, melt the butter until it is popping hot and fry the catfish in the hot butter for 3 minutes on each side, or until the fish flakes easily. Serve hot. Serves 6.

Lagniappe: Be sure that you have a strong vent over your stove if you cook the fish indoors. I don't suggest doing more than the six filets because as the butter will burn from more use. I like to cook this dish outdoors since it does create a lot of smoke. Catfish has a delicate flesh so it cooks quickly. Be sure to coat each filet as evenly as possible.

Carbs per serving: trace
Net carbs per serving: trace
Calories per serving: 326

TROUT LANNETTE

butter to grease bottom of dish
6 trout filets, 6 oz. each
1½ tsp. Seafood Seasoning Mix (see p. 17)
½ cup unsalted butter and melted
1½ tbsp. lemon juice

1 tbsp. dry white wine
2 cloves garlic, very finely minced
1 tsp. Tabasco® Sauce
½ cup chives, finely chopped
1 tsp. fresh basil, minced
1 tsp. Paprika

Preheat the oven to 350 degrees. Grease the bottom of a non-stick baking dish large enough to hold the six filets. Place the fish on the pan and season them well with the Seafood Seasoning Mix. In a small saucepan over medium heat, add the butter, lemon juice, wine, garlic, and Tabasco® Sauce. Heat for 3 minutes, then let it sit for 3 more minutes. When the waiting time has expired, spoon the mixture over each of the filets, then cover each filet equally with the chives, basil, and paprika. Bake the fish for 30 minutes at 350 degrees. Baste the fish a few times with sauce from the bottom of the pan while the fish is baking. Serve immediately, with a little sauce from the pan. Serves 6.

Lagniappe: You can find trout at the supermarket. The key will be to find filets that are uniform in size and weight. You might have to pick and choose, unless you can get rainbow trout or farm-raised trout, which are more uniform in size. You can get the fish completely ready to bake and refrigerate the dish until you are ready to cook. You might have to add a few minutes to the cooking time when you take the fish right from the refrigerator.

Carbs per serving: 2.0 g.
Net carbs per serving: 1.9 g.
Calories per serving: 483

BROILED REDFISH FILETS

6 redfish filets, 8 oz. each
1½ tsp. Seafood Seasoning Mix (see
    p. 17)
1 stick unsalted butter

Preheat the oven to broil. Rinse the fish with cold water and pat dry with paper towels. Season equally with the Seafood Seasoning Mix. Melt the butter in a small saucepan and rub each filet generously with the butter. Pour the remaining butter into a shallow broiling pan and place the 6 filets on top of the butter. Broil about 3 or 4 inches from the heat for 5 minutes on each side. Serve immediately, hot. Serves 6.

Lagniappe: This is as easy as it gets! Redfish is meant to be broiled. There is no need to do anything in advance because it's so easy to do. The only thing that can add to the delicious flavor is to top the dish with Sautéed Lump Crabmeat (see p.158 for the recipe). Just spoon about ½ cup of the crabmeat onto of each filet and you'll have an elegant meal. Bon Appetite!

Carbs per serving: trace
Net carbs per serving: trace
Calories per serving: 425

Carbs per serving with crabmeat: trace
Net carbs per serving with crabmeat:
    trace
Calories per serving with crabmeat: 483

REDFISH EUPHEMIE

6 redfish filets, 6 oz. each
1 tsp. salt
1 tsp. black pepper
½ tsp. cayenne pepper
½ tsp. dried basil
2 tbsp. extra virgin olive oil
3 medium tomatoes, chopped
1 large bell pepper, chopped
1 cups green onions, chopped

¼ cup celery, minced
¼ cup of green olives, sliced
¼ cup of black olives, slice
2 medium jalapenos, chopped
4 cloves garlic, minced
½ cup of fresh squeezed lime juice
3 tbsp. green olive juice
¼ cup fresh parsley, minced
6 thin slices of lime

Preheat the oven to 400 degrees. Rinse the redfish filets under cold water then pat them dry with a paper towel. Mix together the salt, peppers, and dried basil until well blended then sprinkle evenly over each of the 6 fish filets. Pour the olive oil onto a baking dish that has a cover and is large enough to hold all 6 redfish filets. Place the fish filets into the pan. Mix together in a large mixing bowl all the remaining ingredients, except for the minced parsley and the 6 lime slices. When the mixture is blended well together, pour on top of the fish filets. Sprinkle with the fresh parsley and place a lime slice on top of each filet. Cover and bake for 30 minutes at 400 degrees. Serves 6.

Lagniappe: This is an easy, but very tasty, dish. It may have a lot of ingredients, but it is quick and easy to make. You can put the dish together in advance and cover and refrigerate for up to 24 hours. It actually improves the flavor of the fish. The flavors blend together well in the refrigerator and only add to the fish's taste. If there are any leftovers, just refrigerate, heat, and serve again. While it is better the first time, it is still quite good reheated.

Carbs per serving: 14.1 g.
Net carbs per serving: 10.8 g.
Calories per serving: 413

ALMOND ROASTED RED SNAPPER

1 tbsp. extra virgin olive oil

6 red snapper filets, ½-inch

1 tbsp. fresh lemon juice

1 tsp. Tabasco® Sauce

2 tbsp. unsalted butter and melted

1 tsp. fresh ground black pepper

½ tsp. salt

1 tsp. fresh basil, finely minced

½ cup thinly sliced almonds

Preheat the oven to 500 degrees. Lightly grease a large shallow baking dish with the olive oil then place the filets on the dish. Sprinkle with the fresh lemon juice. Mix together the Tabasco® Sauce and the butter, then generously brush the filets with the butter. Season the fish with the pepper, salt, and basil. Sprinkle the almonds over each fish filet. Bake at 500 degrees for 5 minutes. Serve immediately. Serves 6.

Lagniappe: What a great way to serve snapper! This fish roasts well. Be sure that your oven is at 500 degrees before you start to bake. The high temperature sears the fish and gives it the nice roasted flavor. You can completely get the fish ready to bake, then refrigerate covered with plastic wrap until you are ready to put into the oven. In fact, I like to get the fish ready in the morning to serve at dinner time. The flavor tends to intensify.

Carbs per serving: 2.3 g.

Net Carbs per serving: 1.2 g.

Calories per serving: 340

BAKED RED SNAPPER ELOISE

6 red snapper filets, 8 oz. each
1 tsp. Seafood Seasoning Mix (see
   p. 17)
butter for greasing the pan
3 tbsp. mayonnaise
1 tsp. Creole mustard
1 tsp. lemon juice

1 tsp. Worcestershire sauce
1 tsp. Tabasco® Sauce
¾ tsp. onion powder
1 clove garlic finely minced
1 tsp. fresh basil, finely minced
½ tsp. cayenne pepper
1 tsp. Paprika

Preheat the oven to 450 degrees. Wash the filets in cold water then pat dry with paper towels. Season each filet with the seasoning mix. Place on a non-stick, lightly-buttered baking dish large enough to hold the 6 filets. In a mixing bowl, add the remaining ingredients, except for the paprika, and blend together well with a wire whisk. Spread this mixture generously on each snapper filet and bake at 450 degrees for 15 minutes or until the fish flakes easily with a fork. Serve hot. Serves 6.

Lagniappe: You can completely get the fish set to cook, then refrigerate until you are ready to bake. Either set the temperature to 475 and bake for 15 minutes or set the temperature to 450 for 20 minutes. I prefer the higher temperature. If you have leftovers, you can refrigerate and reheat the fish in the microwave. You will lose very little quality, but you do lose a little texture. I actually do like this dish cold, right from the fridge, if I have leftovers. It is an excellent cold fish.

Carbs per serving: .9 g.
Net carbs per serving: .6 g.
Calories per serving: 363

RED SNAPPER YOLANDE

6 red snapper filets, 8 oz. each
1½ tsp. Seafood Seasoning Mix (see
  p. 17)
1 14.75 oz. can stewed tomatoes
¼ cup celery, chopped
2 cloves garlic, minced

¼ cup bell pepper, diced
1 tsp. fresh rosemary
1 tsp. fresh oregano
½ cup feta cheese, crumbled
½ cup Romano cheese, grated

Preheat the oven to 375 degrees. Season the filets with the seasoning mix and place them in a baking dish large enough for each filet to lie flat. In a medium saucepan over medium heat, add the remaining ingredients except for the cheeses; heat together for three minutes. Pour over the fish and sprinkle with the two cheeses and bake for 30 minutes at 375 degrees. Serve hot. Serves 6.

Lagniappe: This is a quick, pour-in-a-pan-and-bake dish. Red Snapper is a tasty fish that bakes well and has a great fresh flavor. Tomatoes have a wonderful affect on the fish. Everyone is sure to rave about this simple dish. They will think you spent lots of time making it. You can completely put this dish together except for the baking and refrigerate for up to 24 hours. Just add 6 extra minutes to the baking time. Actually, it tastes a little better, since the flavors have a tendency to blend fully. Either way, it's a winner.

Carbs per serving: 7.3 g.
Net carbs per serving: 6.4 g.
Calories per serving: 380

RED SNAPPER CHRISTINE NOELIE

1 pound red snapper filets (about 6 filets)

1 tsp. salt

1 tsp. fresh ground black pepper

¼ tsp. cayenne pepper

¼ cup unsalted butter

2 tbsp. extra virgin olive oil

¼ cup lemon juice, freshly squeezed

3 cloves garlic, finely minced

2 tsp. fresh oregano

3 medium tomatoes, ripe and firm, slice

¼ cup fresh parsley, finely minced

Preheat the oven to 400 degrees. Rinse the snapper filets in ice-cold water and pat them dry with paper towels. Season both sides of the filets with the salt, black pepper, and cayenne pepper. Place into a shallow, glass baking dish, just large enough to hold the filets. In a saucepan, combine the butter, olive oil, lemon juice, and oregano. Heat over medium heat for 3 minutes, stirring constantly, then pour over the snapper filets. Place the sliced tomatoes over the snapper filets then spread evenly the fresh parsley. Bake at 400 degrees for 20 minutes or until the fish are flaky and easily cut with a fork. Serve hot immediately. Serves 6.

Lagniappe: You can prepare this dish completely in advance except for baking and set aside for up to 24 hours until you are ready to bake. This is an excellent main dish—easy and tasty. You can freeze for later use, although the dish is better when served fresh right after cooking. Fish does freeze well, but texture of the tomatoes will deteriorate after freezing. I do like this dish cold, too. Leftovers are really great.

Carbs per serving: 4.3 g.
Net Carbs per serving: 3.5 g.
Calories per serving: 320

SAUTÉED SALMON STEAKS

4 center cut salmon filets, 8 oz. each
1 tsp. Seafood Seasoning Mix (see p. 17)
¼ cup soy sauce
¼ cup dry white wine
1 tsp. Tabasco® Sauce

1 tsp. white wine vinegar
1 tbsp. shallots, finely minced
2 cloves garlic, finely minced
2 tbsp. lemon juice, fresh
2 tsp. Splenda® sweetener
¼ cup extra virgin olive oil

Rinse the salmon steaks under cold water, then pat dry with a paper towel. Season equally with the Seafood Seasoning Mix and set aside for later use. Mix together in a large, glass mixing bowl the soy sauce, white wine, Tabasco® Sauce, vinegar, shallots, garlic, lemon juice, and Splenda® until well blended. Place the seasoned salmon steaks in the marinade and marinate for at least 2 hours. When ready to cook, heat a medium skillet over medium-high heat and add the olive oil. When the oil is hot, but not smoking, add the salmon steaks and sauté for 2 ½ minutes on each side. The fish should start to flake but still be quite moist. Serve immediately. Serves 4.

Lagniappe: Salmon is a great fish to cook and eat. It cooks fast and is quite flavorful, especially when marinated. I'm a big fan of salmon when it is seasoned well. Very often salmon is not seasoned. To me, it is so much better with blended seasoning to bring out the flavor of the fish. You can marinate for 24 to 36 hours if you like. It is a quick recipe, after the marinating is complete. Enjoy.

Carbs per serving: 2.9 g.
Net carbs per serving: 2.5 g.
Calories per serving: 613

SALMON STEAKS WITH HOLLANDAISE

3 cups water
1 tbsp. lemon juice
1 tsp. Tabasco® Sauce
1 tsp. salt

4 salmon steaks, 6 oz. each
1 recipe of Hollandaise Sauce (see
   p. 23)

In a 12-inch heavy skillet, add the water and bring to a boil. Add the lemon juice, Tabasco® Sauce, and salt; stir together well. Place the salmon in the boiling water, then reduce the heat to a simmer. Cover and cook for 6 minutes. Test for doneness by checking with a fork; the fish should flake easily. Remove to four warm plates. Cover generously with Hollandaise Sauce or serve with sauce on the side. Serve immediately. Serves 4.

Lagniappe: This is elegant eating. Hollandaise dresses up any dish. The richness of the sauce is a perfect compliment to the pure taste of fish. Salmon is an easy fish to cook. It's fast and simple; all you are doing is poaching the fish. I don't recommend doing anything in advance, except making the Hollandaise Sauce, which can be made up to two hours before you need it and left at room temperature.

Carbs per serving: 1.8 g. with 2 tbsp. Hollandaise
Net Carbs per serving: 1.7 g. with 2 tbsp. Hollandaise
Calories per serving: 380 with 2 tbsp. Hollandaise

CAJUN SALMON SALAD

1 7¾-oz. can salmon, drained
4 hard boiled eggs, chopped
¼ cup celery, diced
¼ cup dill pickle relish
⅛ cup red bell peppers, diced
2 green onions, cleaned and minced
1 tsp. Seafood Seasoning Mix (see p. 17)

¾ cup mayonnaise
1 tbsp. Dijon style mustard
12 spears fresh asparagus, steamed and chopped
lettuce to serve with the salad

In a large mixing bowl, mix together all the ingredients except the lettuce. Spread a bed of lettuce on 4 plates and spoon ¼ of the mixture on to each bed of lettuce. Serve cold. Serves 4.

Lagniappe: This is an easy and tasty salad. You can substitute canned tuna for the salmon and make a wonderful Cajun Tuna Salad (see p. 174). For a bit of variety, you can place the salad on the middle of a leaf of lettuce and make a roll-up with the lettuce forming a wrap for the salad. It is a low-carb way to serve your salad. You can eat either of these salads like you would any salmon or tuna salad. It is excellent when made and served from the serving dish just after it has been blended, but it can be refrigerated and stored for up to 4 days. Seafood salads are an excellent way to start to any good low-carb diet.

Carbs per serving: 6.3 g.
Net carbs per serving: 3.3 g.
Calories per serving: 538

GRILLED SALMON STEAKS

1 medium tomato, seeded and diced
½ grapefruit, peeled and diced
½ navel orange, peeled and diced
½ onion, diced
½ cup red bell pepper, diced
1 medium cayenne pepper, seeds removed and minced

2 cloves garlic, finely minced
¼ cup of fresh parsley, minced
3 tbsp. extra virgin olive oil
3 tbsp. balsamic vinegar
1 tsp. Seafood Seasoning Mix (see p. 17)
4 salmon steaks, 6 oz. each

In a medium bowl add the tomato, grapefruit, orange, onion, bell pepper, and cayenne pepper; stir well together and refrigerate overnight for later use. In another mixing bowl add the remaining ingredients and stir well. Place the salmon steaks in a small shallow baking dish, cover with half of the marinating liquid, and marinate overnight or 8 to 12 hours, turning a few times. Pour the remaining half into the bowl with the fruit and tomatoes then cover and return it to the refrigerator.

When you are ready to grill, brush the salmon with the basting liquid and grill about 10 inches from the heat for 7 to 10 minutes. Place on a warm plate and cover with the reserved tomato/fruit mixture and serve. Serves 4.

Lagniappe: This is a wonderful, exciting, and flavorful way to eat salmon. Salmon doesn't have a lot of flavor on its own, so using imagination adds to the flavor of the fish and enhances the dining experience. The fruit and tomatoes blend well together; it's a different way to serve and you'll get heaps of praise for the dish. See note about balsamic vinegar on page 53.

Carbs per serving: 9.5 g.
Net Carbs per serving: 7.5 g.
Calories per serving: 475

FRESH TUNA À LA RASPBERRY SAUCE

4 tuna steaks, 6 oz. each
1 tsp. Seafood Seasoning Mix (see
   p. 17)
1 tbsp. soy sauce

½ recipe of Raspberry Sauce (see
   p. 44)
2 tbsp. fresh parsley, finely minced
2 tbsp. green onions tops, finely minced

Rinse the tuna steaks in cold water, then pat them dry with a paper towel. Season the steaks with the seasoning mix and place them on a large plate. Sprinkle the soy sauce equally on each steak and set aside. Heat the Raspberry Sauce until it is warm. Heat the grill to hot, and grill each steak for about 3 minutes on each side. Remove to serving plates and cover with about ¼ cup of Raspberry Sauce. Sprinkle the plate and steaks with both the parsley and green onion tops and serve. Serves 4.

Lagniappe: Cooking fresh tuna is easy, quick, and delightful. It is so to be able to find such good-quality, fresh seafood in the grocery store now. Not so long ago, a variety of high-quality fresh seafood was not so readily available. There is no need to do anything for this recipe in advance; it's so quick and easy. You can substitute mahi mahi for the tuna to make Mahi Mahi a la Raspberry Sauce or you can make Salmon a la Raspberry Sauce by using salmon instead of tuna. Either way, just follow the recipe as above. These make wonderful alternatives for your favorite fish.

Carbs per serving: 11.8 g.
Net Carbs per serving: 7.2 g.
Calories per serving: 791

Note: While I like lots of sauce on my fish, you can significantly lower the carb count by using only 2 tbsp., resulting in the following counts:

Carbs per serving: 6.2 g.
Net carbs per serving: 3.8 g.
Calories per serving: 515

FRESH TUNA BAYOU LA COMBE

6 tuna steaks (6 oz. each)

2 tbsp. extra virgin olive oil

1½ tsp. Seafood Seasoning Mix (see p. 17)

¼ cup Seafood Stock (see p. 89) or chicken broth

2 tbsp. white wine vinegar

2 tbsp. dry white wine

2 tbsp. soy sauce

1 tsp. ThickenThin Not/Starch® thickener

2 tbsp. red bell pepper, diced

1 clove garlic, minced

½ cup of green onion bottoms, thinly sliced

¼ cup fresh parsley, minced

Rinse the tuna under cold water and pat dry with a paper towel. Rub the fish generously with the olive oil and season with the seasoning mix. Place the tuna on a hot grill and cook for 3 minutes on both sides, then remove to warm plates. While the fish are grilling, add the stock, vinegar, white wine, soy sauce, and thickener to a medium saucepan and stir well. Heat over medium heat, stirring constantly until the sauce thickens. Add the remaining ingredients, stir in well, and cook for 2 minutes. Pour the sauce over the fish steaks and serve. Serves 6.

Lagniappe: Tuna steaks are made to be grilled. While this dish is best right from the grill, leftovers can be refrigerated for later use. In fact, cold tuna is really quite tasty. When I have leftovers, I mostly eat them chilled rather than heating again. It's almost like you have a different dish.

Carbs per serving: 2.5 g
Net carbs per serving: 1.5 g
Calories per serving: 371

PAN-GRILLED AHI TUNA

6 Ahi tuna steaks, 6 oz. each
2 tbsp. fresh lime juice
1 large red bell pepper, julienned
1 large bell pepper, julienned
1 large onion, slice lengthwise

2 cloves garlic, finely minced
6 green onions, chopped
¼ cup sherry wine
¼ cup pickapepper sauce
1 tsp. Tabasco® Sauce

Rinse the tuna with cold water and pat dry with a paper towel. Sprinkle the lime juice over the tuna and refrigerate for 6 hours. Place the steaks in the bottom of a metal baking dish, cover with the red bell pepper, bell pepper, onion, garlic and green onions. Mix together the wine, pickapepper sauce, and Tabasco® Sauce until well blended. Pour the sauce over the fish. Cover the pan with foil and add to the grill. Cook for 35 to 45 minutes. The fish should flake when touched with a fork and the vegetables should be soft but whole. Serve hot. Serves 6.

Lagniappe: This is another easy dish that flavors tuna well. This can be completely put together before grilling and refrigerated for up to two days before cooking. Just add about 10 minutes to the grilling time. Fresh tuna is wonderful to cook, and is tasty both hot or cold.

Carbs per serving: 16.6 g.
Net carbs per serving: 10.2 g.
Calories per serving: 376

MAHI MAHI SAUCE ROUGE

4 steak of Mahi Mahi, 6 oz. each
¼ cup extra virgin olive oil
1 tsp. salt
1 tsp. black pepper
¼ tsp. cayenne pepper

¼ tsp. sweet basil, dried
½ recipe of Sauce Rouge (see p. 34)
¼ cup of green onions, finely minced
¼ cup of fresh parsley, very finely minced

Rinse the fish steaks in cold water and pat them dry with a paper towel. Rub the steaks with the olive oil until well covered, then mix together the salt, black pepper, cayenne, and sweet basil until well blended and season each steak equally with the seasonings. Grill the steaks for 5 minutes on each side over medium-high heat. Place two tablespoons of Sauce Rouge on each center of four warmed plates and put each filet of mahi mahi on top of the sauce. Sprinkle with a little finely minced green onion tops and fresh minced parsley. Serve immediately. Serves 4.

Lagniappe: Simple yet elegant! Mahi Mahi is such a great fish steak to work with. It has a firm flesh that grills well and has a wonderful flavor. You can rub with the olive oil and season, then refrigerate for up to 24 hours in advance. However, this is such a quick and easy recipe, the only thing you should do in advance is make the Sauce Rouge. Do not plan on serving leftovers because the fish does tend to dry out if not served right from the grill. Enjoy!

Carbs per serving: 6.1 g.
Net Carbs per serving: 4.4 g.
Calories per serving: 692

EGGPLANT CASSEROLE JUSTIN

2 medium eggplants
½ cup heavy whipping cream
½ cup Monterey Jack cheese, shredded
½ cup Swiss cheese, grated
2 low-carb tortillas, finely chopped
1 cup green onions, chopped
½ cup bell pepper, diced
2 tbsp. celery, minced
2 cloves garlic, minced

1 tsp. Seafood Seasoning Mix (see p. 17)
1 tsp. fresh basil, minced
1 tsp. Tabasco® Sauce
¼ cup fresh parsley, minced
1 pound lump crabmeat
2 cups of boiled shrimp, peeled and deveined
1 cup of oysters, drained well (optional)

Peel one of the eggplants and chop both of them into cubes. Place the eggplant in boiling water and cook for 12 minutes, covered. Remove from the heat and let the eggplant stand in the water until you are ready for it. Preheat the oven to 350 degrees. In a large mixing bowl add all the remaining ingredients and stir well. Drain the eggplant and fold into the bowl with the remaining ingredients. Pour into a 2½ quart, lightly-greased baking dish and bake for 35 minutes. Remove and serve immediately. Serves 8.

Lagniappe: This is the perfect dish for eggplant lovers, but it is also a dish anyone will enjoy. While there is lots of eggplant, the dish has so many flavors in it that it's delicious no matter what your favorite food is. You can make this dish completely in advance and refrigerate for up to 3 days before serving. The flavors will intensify in the refrigerator. Just bake at 300 degrees until it is warm and serve as above. What a great dinner.

Carbs per serving without oysters: 10.3 g.
Net carbs per serving without oysters: 5.8 g.
Calories per serving without oysters: 243

Carbs per serving with oysters: 11.5 g.
Net carbs per serving with oysters: 7.0 g.
Calories per serving with oysters: 263

Meats

SAUSAGE AND EGGPLANT

1½ pounds smoked rope pork sausage
3 cloves garlic, minced
2 tbsp. celery, minced
1 large yellow onion, chopped
1 large bell pepper, chopped

¼ cup extra virgin olive oil
2 medium sized eggplant, washed and cut into 1 inch cubes
1 tsp. Cajun Seasoning Mix (see p. 20)
¼ cup fresh parsley, minced

Cut the sausage into thin slices and set aside. In a large skillet over medium-high heat, add the olive oil and let it get hot enough to start popping. Add the sliced sausage, garlic, celery, and onion. Sauté for 4 minutes. Add the bell pepper, eggplant, and seasoning mix and sauté for 15 minutes, stirring frequently. Add the fresh parsley and sauté for one more minute. Serve right from the skillet. Serves 6.

Lagniappe: This is the dish for those of you who like eggplant. The eggplant flavors come alive as the consistency thickens and make the dish tasty and unique. You can make this dish totally in advance and refrigerate for up to 4 days. I like it hot right from the skillet, but I also like to eat it cold right from the fridge. You can use this as a main dish or as a vegetable side dish. I like to serve it over baked chicken breast for a great dressy main dish.

Carbs per serving: 12.7 g.
Net carbs per serving: 10.5 g.
Calories per serving: 524

SAUSAGE ON A STICK

1 lb. pure pork rope sausage sausage, cut into 18 pieces

6 wooden skewers

6 large mushrooms

1 medium green bell pepper, cut into 6 pieces

1 medium onion, cut into 6 wedges

2 ribs celery, cut into 12 pieces

1 medium red bell pepper, cut into 6 pieces

1 tsp. Cajun Seasoning Mix (see p. 20)

¼ cup soy sauce

1 tbsp. Worcestershire sauce

½ tsp. Tabasco® Sauce

Put together 6 shish kabobs by placing a piece of sausage, a mushroom, a slice of bell pepper, a wedge of onion, and a rib of celery on a wooden skewer. Then place another piece of sausage, red bell pepper, a piece of celery, and finally another piece of sausage on the same skewer. Repeat the process until all 6 skewers are used. Sprinkle with the seasoning mix. Mix together the soy sauce, Worcestershire, and Tabasco® and blend well. Baste well with the sauce mixture and grill about 5 inches from the heat source until the sausage is cooked, about 10 minutes. Keep basting during the cooking process. Serve immediately. Serves 6.

Lagniappe: This is a delicious dish you can make in just minutes. Serve it with a heaping of fresh broccoli with hollandaise. You'll have a nice meal. You can cook this on a gas grill or any grill. It does so well and cooks quickly.

Carbs per serving: 8.5 g.
Net carbs per serving: 7.5 g.
Calories per serving: 290

SUMMER PIZZA

2 low-carb tortillas
¼ cup cream cheese
¼ cup pork sausage, cut into pieces
1 green onion, minced
½ cup diced fresh tomatoes

2 tbsp. cooked bacon, crumbled
2 cloves garlic, minced
2 tbsp. bell pepper, diced
½ cup mozzarella cheese, grated
1 tsp. Romano cheese

Preheat the oven to 400 degrees. Spread the cream cheese on each low-carb tortilla. Sprinkle evenly with the sausage, green onion, tomato, bacon, garlic and bell pepper. Top with mozzarella and sprinkle the Romano cheese and Italian seasonings. Bake for 5 minutes or until the mozzarella has melted. Remove from the oven and cut into quarters. Serve hot. Serves 2.

Lagniappe: Here you can be as creative as you like. Use the meat that you want on a pizza and the vegetables as well. You can use tomato sauce if you like, but be sure to use the no-sugar-added and low-carb variety. If you do use sugar-free sauce, just add about 1 or 2 packs of Splenda® to the sauce and it'll taste like the real thing. This dish has unlimited possibilities as long as you choose low-carb choices.

Carbs per serving: 15.8 g.
Net carbs per serving: 8.1 g.
Calories per serving: 471

LOW-CARB JAMBALAYA

2 tbsp. unsalted butter

1 cup ham, diced

½ lb. smoked spicy andouille pork sausage (or any spicy smoked sausage)

1½ cups onions, finely chopped

1 cup red bell pepper, diced

3 cloves garlic, minced

2 cups mushrooms, sliced

1 cup Beef Stock (see p. 86) or beef broth

¼ cup dry white wine

1 tsp. Tabasco® Sauce

½ tsp. salt

1 tsp. black pepper

4 cups cabbage, sliced about ¾-inches wide

½ cup toasted pecans

¼ cup parsley, minced

¼ cup heavy whipping cream

¼ cup sour cream

Heat a 4-quart saucepan over medium-high heat until it is hot, then add the butter and let it melt. When the butter is hot, add the ham and sausage and sauté for 5 minutes, stirring often. Add the onions, bell pepper, and garlic and sauté for 3 more minutes. Then add the mushrooms and sauté for 2 minutes, stirring constantly. Add the remaining ingredients except for the parsley, cream, and sour cream. Bring the mixture to a low boil, then reduce to simmer and cook for 5 minutes, stirring constantly. Add the remaining ingredients and blend in well. Cook for 2 more minutes, stirring constantly. Take care not to let the mixture come to a boil. Serve immediately. Serves 6.

Lagniappe: This recipe is a jambalaya without the carbs or rice. You can substitute the meats of your choice. I like to use leftover meats to make my jambalayas. That's really how the early Cajuns did it; jambalaya was whatever was left in the "ice box." It might have seafood, chicken, pork or beef or even all four mixed together. So really your imagination is the key to what to use. I like the use of cream and sour cream in this recipe because, with cabbage as the starch substitute, the cream and sour cream add a little consistency to the dish.

Carbs per serving: 10.6 g,
Net carbs per serving: 7.3 g.
Calories per serving: 347

CROCKPOT BEEF STEW

3 pounds stew meat, beef

1 3-oz. can tomato paste

2 cups water

½ cup dry red wine

2½ tsp. Beef Seasoning Mix (see p. 19)

3 cloves garlic, minced

1 large onion, chopped

1 large bell pepper, chopped

1 cup celery, chopped

2 turnips, cut into quarters

4 carrots, chopped into thirds

½ cup fresh parsley

Stew meat should be in bite size pieces. Put all ingredients into a large crock pot; stir together and cover. Let cook in the crock pot for at least 8 hours. Serve hot. Serves 8.

Lagniappe: What a wonderful dish to get together the night before you need it. Just turn the crock pot on and forget about it. You'll come home to a wonderful supper. Your whole house will fill with the wonderful smell of a delightful stew. You'll start to wonder why you ever go out for a meal when you can cook up something this good and do it so easily. Be sure to serve this dish in a bowl with a large spoon to be able to enjoy the stock as well as the meat and vegetables. An excellent dish!

Carbs per serving: 15.8
Net carbs per serving: 11.6
Calories per serving: 442

BEEF STROGANOFF

2 pounds boneless sirloin steak, cut into 1½-inch cubes

2 tsp. Beef Seasoning Mix (see p. 19)

1 tbsp. extra virgin olive oil

1 cup onions, chopped

2 cloves garlic, minced

2 tbsp. celery, minced

1 pound mushrooms, sliced

2 cups Beef Stock (see p. 86) or beef broth

2 tbsp. soy flour

1 tbsp. Worcestershire sauce

1 tsp. Tabasco® Sauce

1 cup sour cream

½ tsp. nutmeg

½ cup dry red wine

Season the beef well with the Beef Seasoning Mix and add the olive oil to a heavy skillet over medium-high heat. When the olive oil is hot and starts to pop, add the steak and sauté it on both sides for 3 minutes or until the steak is cooked. If you need to make room for more steak, take the cooked steak and set on a warm plate until all the steak is cooked. Place the steak on a warm plate while you sauté the vegetables. Add the onions, garlic, celery, and mushrooms to the skillet and sauté them for 5 minutes, stirring often. When the vegetables are done, put the steak back in the skillet and add the Beef Stock. Reduce the heat to simmer and cook the meat covered for about 1 hour. Mix together the soy flour, Worcestershire sauce, Tabasco® Sauce, sour cream and nutmeg until well blended. When the steak has cooked for 1 hour add the sour cream mixture and the red wine and stir together well. Continue to cook over a low simmer for 20 more minutes, taking care not to let the Stroganoff boil. Serve hot. Serves 8.

Lagniappe: You can eat this as a soup or as a main dish. I like to serve it over low-carb noodles, but you can also serve it over whipped cauliflower. Actually, I do like to just eat this as a soup. It's so savory and filling. Most of the time, I just like the meat and sauce by itself. It allows me to feel that I'm having the food that I want without the carbs—and, really, it's the meat and sauce that I always liked anyway. Enjoy!

Carbs per serving: 6.1 g
Net carbs per serving: 5.1 g.
Calories per serving: 333

MARINATED GRILLED STEAK

½ cup fresh lemon juice

½ cup Worcestershire sauce

3 tbsp. peanut oil

1 shallot, finely minced

3 cloves garlic, finely minced

¼ cup green onions, finely minced

2 tbsp. fresh ginger, minced

1 tsp. salt

1 tsp. fresh ground black pepper

1 tbsp. fresh basil, finely minced

2 pounds top round steak, about 2 inches thick

In a large bowl, mix all the ingredients except for steak and stir well. Place the steak into the liquid and coat well on both sides. The steak should be partially covered with the marinade. Tightly cover and marinate overnight in the refrigerator. When you are ready to grill, turn the grill on high and then remove the steak from the marinade. Grill for 30 minutes, turning the steak over a few times during the cooking process. Use some of the marinade to baste the steak every time you turn it over. When it is cooked, remove to a serving platter and slice across the grain into thin slices about ½-inch thick. Serve immediately. Serves 6.

Lagniappe: This is a steak lover's dream. The marinade will make the steak tender and juicy and full of flavor. This is the ultimate low carb meal. There is only a trace amount of carbs in each serving. Just a few of the carbs from the marinade make it through to the dish, so you are left with basically just the meat!

Carbs per serving: trace
Net Carbs per serving: trace
Calories per serving: 412

EASY ROAST BEEF

1 beef roast, 7 lb.
3 cloves garlic, quartered
½ shallot, cut into 9 pieces
¼ small bell pepper, cut into 10 pieces
½ small cayenne pepper, cut into 3 pieces

2 tsp. Cajun Seasoning Mix (see p. 20)
2 cups onions, coarsely chopped
½ cup red bell pepper, julienned
1 cup dry red wine
1 cup Beef Stock (see p. 86) or beef broth
¼ cup fresh parsley, minced

Preheat the oven to broil. Stuff the roast with the garlic, shallot, bell pepper, and cayenne by making small cuts in the roast with a sharp knife and forcing the vegetables into the holes with your finger. Season the roast with the Cajun Seasoning Mix. Put the roast in a roasting pot and place under the broiler, uncovered, for 15 minutes. You might think you are burning it, but you don't have to worry; it's just browning. Reduce the temperature to 325 degrees and cook the roast for 2 hours. Remove the roast from the oven, take it out of the pot, and reserve on a warm plate. Place the roasting pot on a high burner and, when the drippings are hot, add the onions and bell pepper. Cook for 3 minutes. Deglaze the pot with the wine and stir well to make sure all the pieces that have stuck to the bottom have dissolved. Cook over high heat for 3 minutes, stirring often. Add the Beef Stock and stir it into the wine until well-mixed. Place the roast back into the pot, cover and cook for 40 more minutes. Remove from the oven. Add the parsley, recover the pot, and let it stand for 5 minutes. Slice and serve warm. Serves 12.

Lagniappe: This is heavy beef at it's best. Each serving is a generous 9 ounces and can be served with any number of wonderful sauces: Béarnaise Sauce, Horseradish Sauce for Beef, Bordelaise Sauce, or Sauce Lyonnaise (all found in the index). Great beef and a great sauce—what a combination. If you want even more variety, you can use 1 cup of strong coffee instead of beef stock, or red wine vinegar instead of the red wine. Each of these liquids will change the taste of the roast, but all of them are delightful to use for deglazing a roast. Try each to see which you like best. Don't be afraid of cooking a roast. It's easy and the end product is real quality. Enjoy!

Carbs per serving: 3.2
Net carbs per serving: 2.8
Calories per serving: 527

STEAK MARIE LOUISE

3 tbsp. olive oil
1 large onion, sliced thin
2 cloves garlic, minced
½ cup Cabernet Sauvignon wine
1½ tbsp. balsamic vinegar
¼ cup Worcestershire sauce
½ cup Beef Stock (see p.xx) or beef broth

3 tsp. Splenda® sweetener
1 tsp. fresh basil, minced
¼ tsp. dried thyme
2 beef rib eye steaks (14 oz. each)
¼ cup fresh parsley, finely minced

Heat olive oil in a large, heavy skillet over medium-high until hot. Separate the onion slices into rings and add them and the garlic to the skillet. Sauté for 7 minutes, stirring occasionally. While the onions are sautéing, add the wine, vinegar, Worcestershire, beef stock, Splenda®, basil, and thyme into a medium mixing bowl. Stir together well and set aside for later use.

Preheat the oven to 250 degrees. After the onions and garlic have sautéed, add the steaks to the skillet and cook them for 5 minutes on each side then remove them to a warm plate. Keep the plate in a 250-degree oven to keep warm until you are ready to serve. Add the liquid mixture that you set aside to the skillet and bring to a gentle boil. Be sure to scrape the bottom of the pan to get any drippings dissolved into the sauce. Cook the liquid for 5 minutes at the low rolling boil stage. Cut the steaks in half and add them to the skillet with the wine sauce. Add the parsley. Cook in the liquid for 2 minutes, turning once. Replate the steaks and serve hot. Serves 4.

Lagniappe: This is a wonderful, full-flavored way to serve steak. You get the great flavor of beef with a sauce that is exceptional. The onions are a nice touch. While this dish is best eaten right after cooking, it can be refrigerated and reheated. The quality is not quite as good, but it is still quite tasty. If you like your steak more rare, just adjust the initial cooking time from 5 minutes per side to 3 minutes per side and continue the recipe as above. See note about balsamic vinegar on page 53.

Carbs per serving: 11.2 g.
Net Carbs per serving: 9.9 g.
Calories per servings: 931

GRILLED BEEF CHUCK STEAK

4 8-oz. boneless beef chuck eye
  steaks, cut 1-inch thick
½ cup red wine vinegar
¼ cup fresh lime juice
3 tbsp. olive oil
3 cloves garlic, finely minced

1½ tsp. Beef Seasoning Mix (see
  p. 86)
½ tsp. fresh ground black pepper
½ tsp. cayenne pepper
⅓ tsp. cumin powder
1 tsp. fresh basil, minced

Place the steaks in a large bowl and add all the ingredients. Stir well to make sure the marinade is well blended. Cover tightly and refrigerate for 12 to 24 hours. Turn the steaks to coat every 2 or 3 hours. When you are ready to grill, turn the grill on high and grill the steaks about 15 inches from the heat. Grill to the doneness you like, about 12 minutes for rare, 15 minutes for medium-rare, and 22 minutes for medium. Place the steaks on a warm individual serving plate and serve with a vegetable or a green salad.

Lagniappe: This is a very flavorful steak. It is usually a little tough, but marinating it overnight will help tenderize it, as well as add additional flavor. This steak is made to be eaten right after being cooked; it does tend to get tough when you try to refrigerate after cooking. Try to cook exactly the amount of steak you need.

Carbs per serving: Trace
Net Carbs per serving: Trace
Calories per serving: 664

GRILLED FLANK STEAK

2 lb. beef flank steak

⅓ cup extra virgin olive oil

⅓ cup fresh lemon juice

¼ cup Worcestershire Sauce

1 tsp. Tabasco® Sauce

4 cloves garlic, finely minced

1 tsp. Beef Seasoning Mix (see p. 86)

1 tsp. fresh ground black pepper

1 tsp. salt

1 tsp. fresh basil, finely minced

Place the beef flank steak in a shallow baking dish to marinate. Combine the remaining ingredients in a medium mixing bowl and blend together well. Pour over the steak, tightly cover and refrigerate for 8 to 12 hours. Turn steak a few times while marinating. When you are ready to grill, get the fire hot and place the grill about 10 inches from the fire or coals. Grill the steak for 12 to 20 minutes, depending on how you want the steak cooked. Twelve minutes for rare, 15 minutes for medium-rare, and 20 minutes for medium. Serve immediately. Serves 4.

Lagniappe: This is a flavorful steak that has to be eaten right after being cooked. The marinate helps to make it tender and give it great flavor. You can chop up any meat that is left to add beef flavor to any vegetable or sandwich.

Carbs per serving: Trace

Net Carbs per serving: Trace

Calories per serving: 760

CAJUN PEPPER STEAK

2 lb. flank steak, slightly frozen
2 egg whites
½ tsp. salt
1½ tsp. Tabasco® Sauce
2 tsp. whole wheat flour
2 tbsp. cooking oil
1 large onion, coarsely chopped
2 small bell pepper, coarsely chopped

2 cloves garlic, minced
½ cup cooking oil
3 tbsp. soy sauce
½ cup Beef Stock (see p. 86) or beef broth
3 tsp. ThickenThin Not/Starch Thickener®

Cut the steak while it is slightly frozen, on the diagonal about ½-inch thick and about 1½-inches long and set aside. Mix together the egg whites, salt, Tabasco® Sauce, flour, and ½ tsp. of cooking oil; beat with a wire whisk until the egg whites begin to foam. When well blended, add sliced steak and work the steak well into the egg mixture with your fingers. Add the onions, bell pepper, and garlic to the steak mixture and blend in well with your fingers. Put ½ cup of cooking oil into a large skillet and heat over medium-high heat until the oil begins to pop, usually about 4 minutes. Put the steak mixture into the hot grease slowly and stir well. Sauté the meat mixture for about 5 minutes at medium-high heat, then add the soy sauce, beef stock, and ThickenThin® thickener. Reduce the heat to medium and cook for 35 to 40 minutes, stirring often. Remove from the heat and serve. Serves 6.

Lagniappe: This steak recipe can be served over low-carb noodles or just eaten as above. I like it by itself with a nice vegetable like broccoli or cauliflower (see the recipe index for recipe ideas). This recipe should be served right after cooking because the meat will be very tender right from the skillet. The onions and bell pepper will be tender, but not too soft, if served immediately. While this dish can be reheated and served as a left-over, it is really best if served right from the skillet. If you do serve over a low-carb pasta, be sure to add the total carbs per serving to the carbs per serving listed below.

Carbs per serving: 8.6 g.
Net Carbs per serving: 6.1 g.
Calories per serving: 736

CHEESY BEEF MELT

2 lb. ground beef, chuck
2 tsp. Beef Seasoning Mix (see p. 19)
1 large onion, finely chopped
3 cloves garlic, minced
1 medium bell pepper, chopped

3 tbsp. celery, minced
1 tsp. Tabasco® Sauce
1 10 ¾-oz. can Rotel diced tomatoes
1½ lb. Velveeta® cheese spread, cut
  into 1-inch blocks

Heat a large skillet over medium-high and add the ground chuck. Sauté for 5 minutes. Reduce the heat to medium and add the Beef Seasoning Mix, onion, garlic, bell pepper, and celery and sauté for 6 minutes. Add the Rotel tomatoes and cook for 2 minutes. Add the cubes of Velveeta® cheese and stir into the meat mixture until all the cheese is dissolved. Serves 8 as an entrée or 20 as a dip.

Lagniappe: This is an easy and quite tasty dish. I use it as an entrée or as a great snack dip. It is good heated or cold as a spread. If you use it as a dip, you can choose to dip your favorite vegetable (low carb, of course). As an entrée you simply can serve it in a bowl or an au gratin dish. Serve any vegetable you like as a compliment. It's also great with or on top of your favorite salad, either with or without the dressing of your choice. I find this a wonderful snack food to keep stored in the refrigerator. It will keep for a full week if refrigerated. I use it as a spread to top various vegetables or to spread onto great low-carb tortillas that are available in most stores (look for tortillas with 3 net carbs or less). Sometimes I even make quick quesadillas by spreading the cheese meat mixture on half of a tortilla and folding it in half. Either heat it in a skillet over low heat just until the cheese begins to melt or for 25 seconds in the microwave. It's a great and filling snack or a super lunch.

Carbs per serving: 13.8 g.
Net Carbs per serving: 12.8 g.
Calories per serving: 653

Carbs per dip serving: 5.5 g.
Net carbs per dip serving: 5.1 g.
Calories per dip serving: 261

TENDERLOIN OF BEEF CAJUN

1½ lb. beef tenderloin, whole and trimmed of excess fat

2 tsp. Cajun Seasoning Mix (see p. 20)

2 tbsp. unsalted butter (not cut into pieces)

2 tbsp. extra virgin olive oil

1 cup green onions, chopped

3 cloves garlic, minced

½ cup turnip, finely minced

2 tbsp. celery, minced

2 tbsp. red bell pepper, diced

½ cup brandy

1 tsp. fresh basil, minced

½ tsp. fresh thyme, minced

1 tsp. Tabasco® Sauce

1 tbsp. Dijon mustard

1 tbsp. medium salsa

1 cup Beef Stock (see p. 86)

2 tbsp. unsalted butter, cut into small pieces and very cold

2 tbsp. fresh parsley, minced

Cut the tenderloin into 4 separate steaks, about 6 oz. each. Season with the Cajun Seasoning Mix and set the steaks aside. In a heavy skillet over medium-high heat, add the butter and olive oil. When the oil is hot, cook the steaks for about 3 minutes on each side for medium-rare or 4 minutes on each side for medium. Remove the steaks to a warm plate, cover loosely with foil, and place in an oven heated to 170 degrees. This will keep the steaks warm, but won't continue to cook them. Add the green onions, garlic, turnips and bell pepper to the skillet and sauté over medium heat for 5 minutes, stirring constantly. Remove from the heat and carefully add the brandy. Return to the heat and ignite the brandy by lighting it with a match, taking care to make sure the pan is stable. Let the flame burn itself out, then add the basil, thyme, Tabasco® Sauce, Dijon mustard, salsa, and Beef Stock. Bring the mixture to a boil, stirring constantly. Cook until the liquid is reduced by about half. The remaining sauce should be somewhat thick. Reduce the heat to low and add the butter piece by piece, whisking it in as you add it, taking care not to boil the liquid or the butter will separate. Stir in the parsley and serve the steaks with a generous amount of the warm Dijon Cajun sauce on top of each steak. Serve immediately. Serves 4.

Lagniappe: Beef tenderloin is an excellent meat to serve for taste and quality. It is low in saturated fats and relatively low in calories. It cooks quickly and is quite tender. Sauces that compliment tenderloin don't have to be heavy or overpowering, but they do need to have quite a bit of depth. I know that a flambé is a problem for many cooks because they are afraid of burning everything down. Just be sure you don't cook on an unstable surface or a pan that is not flat or hard to handle. In order to get the unique flavor of this dish, you do need to flambé it. The burning leaves a tasty residue that gives the dish its unique flavor. Just be careful when lighting the dish and you'll be okay. Don't try to do anything fancy or stir the dish while the flame is burning. This is another "wow!" dish that will amaze your guests. Remember to just let the flame die down by itself and don't use more brandy than the recipe calls for! Have fun. The calories assume you will each eat ¼ of the sauce completely, which rarely happens.

Carbs per serving: 5.6 g.
Net Carbs per serving: 5.2 g.
Calories per serving: 543

FILET OF BEEF WITH SAUCE "J.B."

½ cup butter, whipped
8 filets of beef, 8 oz. each
2 tsp. Beef Seasoning Mix (see p. 19)
1 recipe of Sauce "JB" (see p. 36)

Preheat the oven to 350 degrees. Cover each filet with the butter and season equally with the Beef Seasoning Mix. Place the filets into a baking pan and bake uncovered to your desired degree of doneness, about 15 minutes for medium. When the filets are cooked place them each on a serving plate and place a generous portion of the Sauce "JB" on the side of the plate. Serve immediately. Serves 8.

Lagniappe: What an easy dish, but yet one that is so delicious and filling. This dish is appropriate for the induction phase of any low carb plan. It is basically beef with a wonderful, tasty sauce. You can use as much or as little of the sauce as you like. All you need with this dish is vegetable of your choice or a nice green salad.

Carbs per serving: 3.5 g.
Net Carbs per serving: 3 g.
Calories per serving: 953

RIBEYE STEAKS WITH BORDELAISE SAUCE

3 ribeye steaks, 12 oz. each
2 tsp. Beef Seasoning Mix (see p. 19)
1 recipe Bordelaise Sauce (see p. 27)

Heat a large, heavy, non-stick skillet over high heat. Season the steaks with the Beef Seasoning Mix and cook for three minutes on one side, then turn the steaks over and cook for 4 more minutes on the other side. Turn the steaks again and cook for 4½ minutes more on medium heat until done to the degree you like them. Cut the steaks in half and keep them warm. Heat up the Bordelaise Sauce in the skillet used to cook the steak until the sauce is warm. Spoon it generously over the top of each half steak. Serve hot. Serves 6.

Lagniappe: Make the Bordelaise Sauce in advance and heat it when the steaks to be ready. This is a quick and easy recipe and a meal good enough for company. You can also grill the steaks on an outside grill should you prefer. Just heat the Bordelaise Sauce in a small saucepan and proceed as above. I like to serve this with the "Mock" Loaded Baked Potato (see p. 240)

Carbs per serving: 1.9 g.
Net Carbs per serving: 1.6 g.
Calories per serving: 701

MOMMA'S ROUND STEAK

1½ lb. round steak, about ¾-inch thick
1½ tsp. Beef Seasoning Mix (see p. 19)
2 tbsp. Worcestershire sauce
1 tbsp. soy sauce
1 tsp. red wine vinegar
2 tbsp. extra virgin olive oil

4 cloves garlic, minced
1 cup onion, chopped
1 cup bell pepper, chopped
½ cup celery, sliced about ¼-inch thick
⅔ cup dry red wine
¼ cup fresh parsley, minced

Cut the steak into 1½-inch square pieces. Season the steak well with the Beef Seasoning Mix and place it in a bowl. Cover it with the Worcestershire sauce, soy sauce, and vinegar. Let it marinate in the refrigerator for 2 hours. When you are ready to cook, heat a large, heavy skillet that has a lid over medium-high until hot. Add the olive oil and sauté all the vegetables except the parsley for 5 minutes. Add the steak and sauté well for 12 minutes, stirring it to make sure both sides brown. Add the red wine and any liquid left from the marinating, cover, and cook for 1 hour. Add the parsley, stir well, and let it simmer for 2 minutes. Serve hot. Serves 6.

Lagniappe: This is great "cheap" steak. When I was growing up, the only kind of steak I knew of was round steak. When mom said we were having steak, we all knew what she meant. Everyone who tried it wondered what that great meat was. They said it was not like any steak they'd ever eaten—it was so tender and tasty. We thought they were crazy. Now I know better!

Carbs per serving: 6.7 g.
Net carbs per serving: 5.3 g.
Calories per serving: 361

CHEESEBURGER STEAK

1 lb. ground chuck

1½ tsp. Beef Seasoning Mix (see p. 19 for the recipe)

½ cup onions, finely chopped

2 cloves garlic, finely minced

4 slices of American cheese, about ¼-inch thick

Season the ground chuck with the Beef Seasoning Mix and, using your hands, work the onions, garlic, and seasoning into the meat. Form the meat into 4 hamburger patties. Heat a large, heavy skillet over medium-high heat. When it is hot, place the meat on the skillet. Cook for 3 minutes, then turn the patty over and cook for 3 minutes on the other side. Turn the burger over again and place a slice of cheese on top of each burger. Turn the heat down to medium-low and cook until the cheese has molded to the top and sides of the burger. Serve hot without a bun. Serves 4.

Lagniappe: I almost hate to put this in the book, but believe it or not, many people don't know how to make a good burger. This is easy and the taste of the beef carries the dish. It's great for lunch or for a light dinner. You can season and mold the burger and refrigerate until you are ready to cook. I do not like to make them in advance because the meat is tastier and more tender if served just after cooking. It cooks so fast that there really is no need to cook it in advance. I like to serve mine with a mixture of mustard and mayonnaise and a nice tomato salad on the side.

Carbs per serving: 2.5 g.
Net carbs per serving: 2.1 g.
Calories per serving: 467

MOSS BLUFF MEATLOAF

2 lb. ground round
2 tsp. Beef Seasoning Mix (see p.19 for recipe)
1 tsp. Tabasco® Sauce
1 tbsp. Worcestershire sauce
1 cup green onions, chopped
3 cloves garlic minced

2 large brown eggs, slightly beaten
1 cup ham, chopped
¼ lb. sharp cheddar cheese, cut into ½-inch cubes
¼ lb. Swiss cheese, cut into ½-inch blocks
1 cup pork skins, crushed

Preheat the oven to 375 degrees. In a large mixing bowl, add the ground round and season it with the Beef Seasoning Mix, Tabasco®, and Worcestershire. Add the remaining ingredients except for the pork skins and work it together good with your hands. Form it into a loaf and place in a 3 lb. meatloaf pan. Top the meatloaf with the pork skins and bake at 375 degrees for 45 minutes. Remove from the oven and let it stand for 5 minutes, then cut into slices and serve. Serves 8.

Lagniappe. This is a meatloaf that you can serve to anyone, even if they are not on a low-carb diet. The taste is wonderful. It can be made in advance, cooked, and refrigerated for later use. Just keep it in the pan until you are ready to serve. Heat it by covering it with foil and warming it at 300 degrees for 10 to 12 minutes, then slice and serve. I also like to use this leftover meatloaf to make Meatloaf Quesadillas by cutting the meat into pieces and following the recipe for Quesadillas (see the index for the recipe). You can also make Meatloaf Sandwich. Take a low-carb tortilla, put a nice slice of meatloaf on one half, add mayonnaise, mustard, pickle, lettuce, and tomato, and fold it in half. What a great sandwich!

Carbs per serving: 1.6 g.
Net carbs per serving: 1.6 g.
Calories per serving: 311

CAJUN CANNON BALLS

1½ lb. ground round
1 tsp. Cajun Seasoning Mix (see p. 20)
2 cloves garlic, minced
1 shallot, finely minced
½ cup bell pepper, finely diced
¼ cup celery, finely minced
2 large eggs, beaten
1 tsp. Tabasco® Sauce
1 tbsp. Worcestershire sauce

¾ cup Beef Stock (see p. 86)
1 8-oz. package cream cheese, softened
   and cubed
1 tbsp. low-carb catsup
¼ cup dry Burgundy wine
1 tbsp. balsamic vinegar
2 tsp. fresh sweet basil, finely minced
1 tbsp. fresh parsley, minced

Preheat the oven to 350 degrees. In a large mixing bowl, add the ground round and season it with the Cajun Seasoning Mix, garlic, and shallots, mixing it lightly together with your hands. Add the bell pepper, celery, eggs, Tabasco® Sauce, and Worcestershire and mix in well with your hands. Form into ¾-inch round meatballs. Place them on a non-stick baking dish; be sure not to let them touch each other. Bake until the meatballs are brown, about 20 minutes. Remove from the oven and let them cool. While the meatballs are cooling, add the remaining ingredients to a large, heavy saucepan over medium heat and cook until the cheese is melted, stirring constantly. Turn the heat to low and put the cooked meatballs into the cheese mixture and carefully stir them into the sauce. Put about half the drippings from the baking dish into the sauce, trying to get as much of the sticky meat drippings as possible. Let the sauce cook over low simmering heat for 10 minutes so the flavors will blend; carefully stir often to prevent sticking. Serve immediately. Serves 6.

Lagniappe: The dish can be made completely in advance and refrigerated or frozen. When you are ready to serve, thaw in the refrigerator, then heat over very low temperature until the meatballs are hot. Any leftovers make great sandwich meat to serve on a low-carb tortilla. You can even put extra cheese and fold the tortilla and heat it in the microwave. See note about balsamic vinegar on page 53.

Carbs per serving: 3.8 g.
Net carbs per serving: 3.4 g.
Calories per serving: 485

JUST GRILLED STEAK

4 steaks (sirloin, ribeye, or Filet Mignon), about 8 oz. each

2 tsp. Beef Seasoning Mix (see p. 19 for the recipe

¼ tbsp. unsalted butter

2 tbsp. Worcestershire sauce

2 tbsp. lemon juice

1 tsp. Tabasco® Sauce

Season the steaks with the seasoning mix. Melt the butter in a small saucepan and add the Worcestershire, lemon juice, and Tabasco®. Stir together well. Brush the marinade on the steaks as you put them on the grill. Cook them about 5 inches from the heat and constantly brush with the butter mixture. Cook for 4 minutes on one side and 5 on the other. Adjust cooking time for doneness. You can press the meat to determine the degree of doneness. The firmer the meat is, the more cooked it will be. If you like medium-rare, the steaks should be cooked. Serve hot. Serves 4.

Lagniappe: This is good low-carb food. It's pure beef, with just a little bit of marinade, so it has only a trace amount of carbs. You can enjoy this meal without guilt. While the pure low-carb dieter believes that it doesn't matter how many calories you eat as long as it's low carb, I believe you should know the calorie count as well to help you understand just what you are eating. The calorie count for this dish is high, so enjoy, but do understand that this is not every-day fare! You can see the calorie difference for the three different kinds of steaks, while the carb and net carb count remains the same. Leftovers make great low-carb sandwich meat. Chop them up and the meat stretches and makes more sandwiches.

Carbs per serving: trace
Net carbs per serving: trace
Calories per ribeye serving: 700
Calories per sirloin serving: 463
Calories per filet mignon serving: 830

CAMPFIRE BOLOGNA

8 oz. Velveeta® cheese, cut into blocks
½ cup celery, sliced about ¼-inch thick
¼ cup onions, chopped
1 tsp. Tabasco® Sauce

½ lb. pork or chicken bologna, cut into ½-inch cubes (or if it's already sliced, cut into ½-inch slices).

In a medium saucepan over medium heat, add all the ingredients and cook until the cheese is melted. Serve immediately without a bun. Serves 4.

Lagniappe: Sounds like the old campfire fun time! Well, that is exactly what it is. It can be done in a home kitchen as well. It's a quick and easy, low-carb treat for lunch or for a late night snack. You can keep the leftovers for later use. To reheat, just heat over low and serve when the cheese is melted. You can also microwave it in a covered dish at 80 percent power for about 1 minute. You can use the same recipe to make Campfire Hot Dogs by substituting 1 lb package of beef frankfurters cut into fourths and following the same recipe.

Campfire Bologna
Carbs per serving: 11.1 g.
Net carbs per serving: 7.6 g.
Calories per serving: 358

Campfire Hot Dogs
Carbs per serving: 8.3 g.
Net carbs per serving: 6.8 g.
Calories per serving: 465

VEAL CHOPS MARCHAND DE VIN

4 veal rib chops (about 1-inch thick bone in), 10 oz each

1 tsp. Beef Seasoning Mix (see p. 19 for the recipe)

1 cup Marchand de Vin Sauce (see p. 30 for recipe)

Preheat the oven broiler. Wash the veal chops in cold water and pat them dry with a paper towel. Season them well with the Beef Seasoning Mix and place the chops on the rack of a broiler pan. Broil about 4 inches from the heat source for 5 minutes, then turn them and broil for 4 more minutes or until desired doneness. Remove from the broiler and keep on a warm plate. Pour the liquid from the bottom of the broiler pan into a saucepan and add the Marchand de Vin Sauce and heat until warm. Spoon the mixture on top of the veal chop or serve it in a sauce boat on the side. Serve immediately. Serves 4.

Lagniappe: This is good for a company dinner or elegant family meal. Serve with your favorite bottle of wine. I like Grilled Vegetables and Creamy "Mock" Potatoes with this dish. You really want to eat this dish right after cooking it. It is at its best when served right away. Enjoy this dish now, because there won't be any leftovers.

Carbs per serving: 3.2 g.
Net carbs per serving: 2.4 g.
Calories per serving: 782

PORK CHOPS DON LOUIS

3 tbsp. unsalted butter
1 cup cabbage, shredded
1 cup onions, chopped
2 cloves garlic, minced
1 tsp. black pepper
2 tsp. Tabasco® Sauce

½ tsp. salt
3 tsp. Cajun Seasoning Mix (see p. 20)
4 center-cut pork chops, 6 oz. each
½ cup sour cream
1 tsp. fresh basil, minced

Preheat the oven to broil. In a large heavy skillet, over medium-high heat add the butter and let it melt and get hot. Sauté the cabbage, onions, garlic, pepper, Tabasco and salt for 7 minutes, stirring often. While the cabbage is sautéing, season the pork chops with the seasoning mix, and place them on a broiling rack about 6 inches from the heat source and broil for 5 minutes on each side. When the cabbage is through sautéing, add the sour cream and basil and mix together well. Spoon equal amounts of the cabbage mixture onto the center of 4 warm plates. Place each of the pork chops on top of the cabbage and serve hot. Serves 4.

Lagniappe: This is such a pretty dish and is loaded with flavor. You get the wonderful taste of roasted port and the creamy flavor of cabbage blended together in one quick dish. This is company food that is easy enough for everyday fare! Do not try to make in advance and refrigerate; the pork and cabbage are both better right after initial cooking. The only thing I ever do in advance is chop my vegetables and have them ready to go.

Carbs per serving: 5.9 g.
Net Carbs per serving: 5 g.
Calories per serving: 520

STUFFED PORK CHOPS MELANCON

4 center cut pork chops, 1-inch thick each

1 tsp. Cajun Seasoning Mix (see p. 20 for the recipe)

½ cup mushrooms, finely chopped

¼ cup fresh parsley, minced

1 tbsp. green onions, finely minced

¼ cup Swiss cheese, grated

1 tbsp. Romano cheese, grated

1 clove garlic, minced

1 tsp. Tabasco® Sauce

1 tsp. Worcestershire sauce

½ tsp. salt

3 tbsp. extra virgin olive oil

½ cup Merlot wine

Season each of the pork chops well with the Cajun Seasoning Mix and slit a hole through one half of the pork chop, away from the bone, to make a nice pocket in each chop. Set aside. Mix together the remaining ingredients, except for the olive oil and wine, until well mixed. Stuff equal amounts of this mixture into the pockets of each chop and press the chop closed. In a heavy, metal, medium skillet, add the olive oil and let it get hot and start to smoke. Add the chops to the skillet and thoroughly brown well on both sides, about 3 minutes on each side. Remove the chops from the pan and deglaze the skillet with the wine, taking care to remove all the pieces that have stuck to the bottom of the pan. Reduce the heat to low and return the chops to the skillet. Cover and simmer for about 40 minutes or until the meat is very tender. Serve hot. Serves 4.

Lagniappe: This makes delicious chops! The stuffing is so good and the meat will be flavored both inside and out. This is a good dish to serve to company. You can stuff the chops in advance and store in the refrigerator until you are ready to cook. I cover them tightly with plastic wrap. You can even freeze them for later use if you like. It's a great idea to have a few of these stuck in your freezer for that last minute surprise dinner party you have to throw. Your guests will think you shopped and worked hard all day!

Carbs per serving: 2.7 g.
Net carbs per serving: 2.4 g.
Calories per serving: 607

CAJUN LOW-CARB SANDWICH

1 low-carb tortilla (3 net carbs)
1 tbsp. mayonnaise
1 tsp. Creole mustard
2 slices deli ham, (about ⅛-inch thick)
1 slice Swiss cheese

1 slice fresh Tomato, cut in half
¼ cup lettuce, shredded
1 tbsp. pickled pepper rings
1 purple onion, sliced thin

Spread the mayonnaise and Creole mustard evenly on the tortilla. Place two slices of ham on top of the mayonnaise and cove the ham with the cheese. Place the two halves of tomato on the sandwich. Cover with the shredded lettuce, pickled pepper, and purple onion. Fold in half and cut in half. Makes one sandwich and serves 1.

Lagniappe: I never thought I'd have to tell people how to make a sandwich, but you can't believe how many people have asked me, "How did you make this?" So I guess I will put it in writing so all will know. Of course, you can do just about anything you want to make your own sandwich. Just remember to count all the carbs! You can make these sandwiches in advance; cover them tightly with plastic wrap and keep them refrigerated. They make quick, easy lunches and the carb-count is great! I just like to fold them over, but you can be creative and fold the tortilla like a burrito if you like. Sometimes I roll it and slice it into fourths. However you like it, it's only for looks, so be creative!

Carbs per serving: 15.9 g.
Net carbs per serving: 6.9 g.
Calories per serving: 329

LOW-CARB CROQUE MONSIEUR

2 tsp. unsalted butter
2 low-carb flour tortillas (3 net carbs
   each)
1 tsp. Dijon mustard
3 slices of deli-ham, about ⅛-inch thick
   each

2 slices Swiss cheese
2 slices Provolone cheese
2 thin slices of large onion, sliced
   ⅟₁₆-inch thick

Heat a medium-sized, non-stick skillet over medium heat and add the butter and let it melt. Lightly spread the Dijon mustard on a tortilla. Place the ham on top of the mustard. Cover the ham with the Swiss cheese and add the 2 slices of onion. Cover the onion with the Provolone and put the remaining tortilla on top of the cheese. Place the sandwich cheese-side down in the skillet with the melted butter. Cook, lightly shaking the pan a few times, for 2 minutes. Carefully flip the Croque Monsieur over and cook the other side in the same manner as the first. Flip it back over and cook for 1 more minute. Slide it onto a serving plate and cut in half with a sharp knife and serve. Serves 1.

Lagniappe: This is a famous French sidewalk dish that you'll find all over Paris. Sometimes it's made with a crepe or with slices of French bread. This recipe uses a low-carb tortilla and you'll almost swear it is a crepe. It's a delight and simple to cook. Even your kids will like it, although you might have to leave the Dijon mustard and onion out.

Carbs per serving: 26.8 g.
Net carbs per serving: 10.2 g.
Calories per serving: 670

QUESADILLAS

4 low-carb tortillas (3 net carbs each)
½ cup Monterey Jack cheese, grated
½ cup American cheese, grated
¼ cup sharp cheddar cheese
1 green onion, chopped
¼ cup red bell pepper, julienned

½ lb. beef roast, sliced thin
2 tbsp. jalapeno peppers cut in circles
2 cloves garlic, minced
2 tbsp. unsalted butter
¼ cup sour cream
spicy salsa as desired

Place two tortillas each on two dinner plates. Spread half of the Monterey Jack cheese evenly on both tortillas. Repeat the process with American cheese and then with the cheddar. Evenly spread the green onions and red bell pepper on each of the two tortillas. Put half of the meat on each tortilla, spreading it out so that most of the tortilla is covered. Sprinkle evenly with the jalapeno and then the garlic. Cover evenly with the cheese, then put the two unused tortillas on top of the cheese. In a medium skillet, melt half of the butter. When melted, slide one prepared quesadilla onto the skillet, taking care not to spill out the insides. Heat over medium heat for 2 minutes, then carefully turn it over. Cook, shaking the skillet gently, for 2 more minutes, then flip it over and cook for 1 more minute. Transfer to a plate and keep it warm (165 to 170 degrees) while you repeat the entire process with the other tortillas, starting with the tablespoon of butter. When you are finished, serve with the sour cream and spicy salsa on the side. Serves 1.

Lagniappe: This is a great evening meal or a wonderful lunch. You can vary the meat to fit your preference. I use sausage, ground meat, chicken strips, turkey or barbecue. You can also vary the cheeses to suit your taste. For that matter you can vary the vegetables used as well. I like to also sauté slices of eggplant in olive oil, just until they get soft then add them to the quesadilla. Sautéed mushrooms or grilled vegetables can be added as well. You can see the possibilities are multiple.

Carbs per serving: 30.1 g.
Net carbs per serving: 13.1 g.
Calories per serving: 1103

LAMB CHOPS PORT ROYAL

8 trimmed rib lamb chops, about ¾-inch thick, 3 oz. each
1¼ Cajun Seasoning Mix (see p. 20 for the recipe)
2 tbsp. extra virgin olive oil
¼ cup unsalted butter
3 cloves garlic, minced

½ cup red bell pepper, julienned
2 medium white onions, sliced into rings and separated
2 tbsp. celery. minced
⅔ cup cognac
2 tbsp. heavy whipping cream
1 tsp. Tabasco® Sauce

Season the chops with the seasoning mix and set them aside. In a large, heavy skillet over medium-high, heat the olive oil until it is hot, then add the butter and melt it until it begins to smoke. Add the garlic and sauté it for 30, stirring often. Add the lamb chops and brown them for 3 minutes on each side. Remove the chops to a warm platter. Add the bell pepper, onions, and celery and sauté for 3 minutes, stirring constantly. Return the chops to the pan and reduce the heat to low. Carefully add the cognac. Strike a match away from the skillet, then bring the match to the skillet. The cognac will ignite with a puff. Be careful at this stage. Let the dish burn itself out. Stir the skillet well to make sure all the stuck pieces on the bottom are dissolved. Serve immediately. Two chops covered with the sautéed vegetables per serving. Serves 4.

Lagniappe: There is nothing you can do in advance, but chop the vegetables. This dish cooks in less than 10 minutes, so it's quick as well as easy. No leftovers for this meal-the food will all be gone. This is definitely a company dish because it's so showy. It'll look like you went to a lot of trouble because it's a flambé. That always tends to impress!

Carbs per serving: 6.7 g.
Net Carbs per serving: 5.6 g.
Calories per serving: 560

Poultry

CHICKEN LAFAYETTE

¼ cup extra virgin olive oil

1½ pounds chicken breast, cut into bite size pieces

2 tsp. Chicken Seasoning Mix (see p. 18)

1 bell pepper, diced

½ cup celery, chopped

½ cup green onions, chopped

1 cup of pepperoni slices

1 large onion, sliced across the grain about ½-inch thick

1 clove garlic, finely minced

¼ cup Parmesan cheese, grated

1 tsp. fresh parsley, minced

In a large heavy skillet over medium-high heat, add the olive oil let it start to smoke. Season the chicken with the seasoning mix and then sauté for 15 minutes or until it is nicely browned. Add the bell pepper, celery, and green onions and sauté for 5 minutes, then add the pepperoni slices and garlic. Sauté for 6 more minutes, stirring constantly. Add the Parmesan cheese and sprinkle with the fresh parsley and serve. Serves 6.

Lagniappe: This looks so simple you might think that it can't be delicious, but don't let it fool you. The flavor of chicken and the taste of pepperoni are delightful together. You can use this same recipe and change the chicken for pork and make Pork Lafayette. Just cut a small pork loin into bite size pieces and follow the recipe as if it were chicken. Either way, you are in for a real treat. You can cook the dish in advance completely and cover or you can make the cream cheese mixture and let it stand until you are ready to serve. This is a tasty low-carb treat to keep stored in the fridge for quick and savory treats any time of the day.

Carbs per serving: 6 g.
Net carbs per serving: 4.6 g.
Calories per serving: 409

CHICKEN CONTI

1 pound chicken breasts
1 tsp. Chicken Seasoning Mix (see p. 18)
1 head fresh broccoli
1 tbsp. unsalted butter
¼ cup onions, finely chopped
1 clove garlic, finely minced
½ cup celery, finely chopped
⅛ cup red bell pepper, finely diced
½ tsp whole wheat flour
1 cup heavy whipping cream
1 tsp. Tabasco® Sauce
½ cup sharp cheddar cheese, grated
½ cup Monterey Jack cheese, grated
2 tbsp. fresh parsley, minced
paprika

Preheat the oven to 375 degrees. Wash the chicken in cold water and pat dry with a paper towel. Cut the chicken into bite-size pieces and season with the seasoning mix. Place in a lightly-greased baking dish (about 12 x 12). Wash and trim the broccoli and cut it into serving-size pieces and arrange it next to the chicken. In a medium heavy skillet over medium heat, add the butter and let it melt and get hot. Sauté the onion, garlic, celery, and red bell pepper for 4 minutes, stirring often. Add the flour and cook for 3 minutes, stirring constantly. Remove the skillet from the heat and add the cream and Tabasco® Sauce, then return to the heat and cook for 3 minutes, stirring often. Pour the cream mixture over the chicken and broccoli. Cover with the two cheeses equally. Sprinkle with parsley and dust lightly with paprika. Bake at 375 degrees for 30 to 40 minutes or until the chicken is cooked. Serve hot. Serves 6.

Lagniappe: This dish can be completely put together for baking at a later date and refrigerated for up to 48 hours before cooking. It can also be completely cooked and refrigerated, tightly covered with plastic wrap, for up to 4 days, then reheated and served. Since you are using raw broccoli, it will hold up nicely after being cooked and then refrigerated. While it can be frozen, I prefer not to. The cream does tend to change its texture after being frozen. The taste is fine, but eye appeal is hurt.

Carbs per serving: 8.6 g.
Net carbs per serving: 4.9 g.
Calories per serving: 398

POULET Á LA CALCASIEU

6 skinless chicken breast halves, about 6 oz. each
1 tsp. Chicken Seasoning Mix (see p. 18 for the recipe)
3 tbsp. extra virgin olive oil
1½ cup onions, coarsely chopped
3 cloves garlic, minced
½ cup bell pepper, diced
½ cup celery, sliced

1½ cup mushrooms, sliced
1 14.5-oz. can tomatoes diced in sauce
½ cup dry Burgundy wine
1 packet Splenda® sweetener
2 tsp. fresh basil, minced
½ tsp. dried oregano
½ tsp. dried rosemary
½ cup Parmesan cheese, grated
1 tbsp. Romano cheese, grated

Cut the chicken breasts into strips and season well with the Chicken Seasoning Mix. In a large skillet over medium-high heat, add the olive oil and let it get hot. When it is hot, fry the chicken until it is nice and browned on all sides, about 12 minutes. Add the onions, garlic, bell pepper, and celery and sauté for 4 minutes over medium-high heat, stirring constantly. Add the mushrooms and sauté them for 1 minute. Add the remaining ingredients except for the cheeses and reduce the heat to simmer. Cook for 30 minutes, stirring occasionally. Add the cheeses and simmer for 1 more minute, then serve. Serves 6.

Lagniappe: I like to eat this dish by itself, but it's also good over steamed cabbage or over lightly sautéed spaghetti squash. The flavors are wonderful. The chicken is tender and you'll find yourself scraping the plate to get every last morsel. You can make it in advance and refrigerate or freeze for later use. To use after freezing, just thaw in the refrigerator and heat over low heat until the chicken is hot, about 15 minutes.

Carbs per serving: 13.8 g.
Net carbs per serving: 7.3 g.
Calories per serving: 600

CHICKEN ENCHILADA CASSEROLE

olive oil flavored baking spray
1 lb. skinless chicken breast
1 tsp. Cajun Seasoning Mix (see p. 20)
2 tbsp. extra virgin olive oil
1 cup onions, chopped
3 cloves garlic, minced
½ cup red bell pepper, diced
1 small can chilies

¼ cup jalapeno slices, chopped
¼ cup black olives, chopped
½ cup half-and-half cream
4 low-carb tortillas (3 net carbs each)
1 cup colby cheese
1 cup Pepper Jack cheese
¾ cup sharp cheddar cheese

Preheat the oven to 350 degrees. Lightly spray a 9 x 9 x 2 ½-inch baking dish with the olive oil spray and set aside. Season the chicken breasts with the Cajun Seasoning Mix, spray a small baking pan with the olive oil spray, and bake the chicken for 20 minutes. While the chicken is baking, add the olive oil to a large skillet over medium-high heat. Add the onions, garlic, red bell pepper, and celery and sauté for 3 minutes. Remove from the heat and add the chilies, jalapeno slices, and black olives and stir together well. Set aside for later use. When the chicken is done, remove it from the oven and chop it into medium sized chunks. Take the 9 x 9 baking dish and place two tortillas in the bottom. Spread half of the chicken on top of the tortillas and cover with half of the sautéed mixture. Pour half of the half-and-half on top and sprinkle with ½ cup of the colby cheese and ½ cup of the Pepper-Jack cheese. Cover with the remaining tortillas and repeat the exact process as listed above. Sprinkle with the sharp cheddar and dust with paprika. Sprinkle the parsley over the dish and bake for 30 minutes at 350 degrees. Remove and let stand for 2 minutes and serve with a large spoon. Serves 6.

Lagniappe: This dish can be made in advance and refrigerated until you are ready to serve. Just cover tightly with plastic wrap. It also freezes well if you can keep the family from eating it before you have a chance to freeze it. I usually like to make a double recipe and eat one and freeze one. That way you'll have a quick meal when you don't have time to cook. It really isn't too difficult to double the recipe and do two at the same time. You can also use the same recipe as to make Beef Enchiladas du Lac Charles. Just use 1½ pound of ground round and follow the same recipe as above, except you will sauté the ground beef in the same skillet you sauté the vegetables. I also like to use fajita meat to make Fajita Enchiladas. I follow the recipe as above, except I season and grill 1 pound of fajita meet on the grill and chop it when it is cooked. No matter how you make them, enchiladas are delicious!

Carbs per serving: 12.2 g.
Net carbs per serving: 5.9 g.
Calories per serving: 317

LIME-ROSEMARY BROILED CHICKEN BREASTS

6 boneless chicken breasts, skin removed, 6 oz. each
¾ cup extra virgin olive oil
¾ cup fresh lime juice

3 cloves garlic, finely minced
3 tbsp. fresh rosemary, chopped
1 tsp. salt
1 tsp. fresh ground black pepper

Preheat the oven to broil. Place each breast of chicken between two sheets of wax paper and pound with the flat side of a meat mallet until the size has increased by about ⅓. In a small mixing bowl, combine the olive oil, lime juice, garlic, and 2 tbsp. of the rosemary. Place the chicken in a flat dish and cover with the olive oil/rosemary mixture. Marinate for at least 2 hours. When you are ready to cook, remove the chicken to a broiling pan, sprinkle the remaining 1 tbsp. rosemary, and season with salt and pepper. Broil the chicken breast for 2½ minutes on each side. Serve immediately. Serves 6.

Lagniappe: This is a simple marinade and the lime juice gives the chicken such a great flavor. Rosemary flavors chicken nicely. My grandmother used to use rosemary on the Sunday chicken. I have always liked the flavor it imparts on the chicken.

Carbs per serving: 1.5 g.
Net Carbs per serving: 1.4 g.
Calories per serving: 380

GREEN PEPPERCORN CHICKEN

2 whole chicken breasts, skin removed
1 tsp. Chicken Seasoning Mix
   (see p. 18)
2 tbsp. Dijon mustard
3 tbsp. extra virgin olive oil
1 cup of mushrooms, diced

½ cup heavy whipping cream
¼ cup dry white wine
2 tbsp. green peppercorns
1 tbsp. balsamic vinegar
1 tsp. Tabasco® Sauce

Cut the chicken breasts in half. Using a meat mallet, flatten each piece of chicken breasts until they have nearly doubled in size. Season evenly with the Chicken Seasoning Mix, and spread the Dijon mustard evenly over each chicken breast half. In a large heavy skillet over medium-high heat, brown the chicken on each side by cooking the chicken at medium-high heat. Take care not to burn the chicken. When the chicken is fully cooked (about 10 minutes), remove to a warm platter. Add the mushroom dices and sauté, stirring often, for 3 minutes. Mix together the remaining ingredients and pour them into the skillet that the chicken was in. Bring the cream mixture to a boil, then reduce the heat to simmer. Cook until the mixture thickens, stirring often. Spoon the peppercorn sauce over the chicken breasts and serve immediately. Serves 4.

Lagniappe: This is a nice afternoon meal or a special dinner. It is easy to cook and the look is spectacular. You can cut and pound the chicken in advance. Everything else should be done right after you start cooking. I do not like to reheat this dish after it has been prepared. See note about balsamic vinegar on page 53.

Carbs. Per serving: 2.8 g.
Net carbs per serving. 2.8 g.
Calories per serving: 540

BREAST OF CHICKEN EMILUS

¼ cup unsalted butter

1½ tsp. Chicken Seasoning Mix (see p. 28)

2 whole chicken breasts, halved, 14 oz. each

2 cloves garlic, minced

1 tbsp. shallots, minced

½ cup red bell pepper, diced

2 tbsp. celery, minced

1 small jalapeno, minced

1 tsp. all purpose flour

½ cup sour cream

1 cup petit pois peas, cooked and drained

¾ cup mushrooms, sliced

2 tbsp. fresh parsley, minced

Heat a large, heavy skillet over medium-high heat until it is hot then add the butter. While the butter is heating, season the chicken with the seasoning mix and place on a cutting board. Cover with plastic wrap and pound the chicken about 5 times with a kitchen mallet (smooth side only). When the butter begins to smoke, sauté the chicken breasts on each side for about 5 minutes. Remove the chicken to a warm platter and set aside for later use. Add the garlic, shallots, bell pepper, and celery and sauté for 5 minutes, stirring constantly. Add the jalapeno and flour and sauté for 3 minutes, stirring constantly. Reduce the heat to low and stir in the sour cream; take care not to boil the sour cream or it will separate. Stir in the peas and mushrooms. Cook over low heat for 2 minutes, stirring often. Add the parsley and blend in well, then return the chicken to the skillet. Simmer over low heat, stirring occasionally. Serve by putting one chicken breast half on each of four plates and cover with the vegetable/cream mixture. Serves 4.

Lagniappe: When it comes to variety, chicken breast is the best meat to use. Chicken can adapt to almost any ingredient and offers a variety in both looks and texture. The end product is always appetizing and appealing. This dish should be eaten right after being cooked. It cooks quickly and, even with a lot of ingredients, it is effortless. Cook it, serve it, and eat it.

Carbs per serving: 9 g.
Net carbs per serving: 7.5 g.
Calories per serving: 599

CHICKEN ETIENNE

1½ lb. skinned boneless chicken breasts
1 tsp. Cajun Seasoning Mix (see p. 20)
3 tbsp. extra virgin olive oil
1 medium onion, cut into wedge chunks
1 medium bell pepper, julienned
3 cloves garlic, minced
½ cup celery, sliced
1 tbsp. all purpose flour
½ cup white wine vinegar

1 cup dry white wine
1 tsp. salt
2 medium fresh ripe tomatoes, skinned and diced
1 tsp. fresh thyme (or ⅓ tsp. dried)
2 tsp. fresh basil, minced
1 tsp. fresh sage, chopped
1 tbsp. Worcestershire sauce
1 tsp. Tabasco® Sauce
1 cup ripe black olives, cut in half

Cut the chicken into 3-inch strips and season with the Cajun Seasoning Mix. Heat a large, heavy skillet over medium-high heat and add the olive oil. When the oil is hot, add the chicken and cook for 5 minutes, stirring often. The chicken should be browned. Add the onions, bell pepper, garlic, and celery and sauté for 5 more minutes, stirring often. Reduce the heat to medium, add the flour and cook for 4 minutes, stirring constantly. Add the vinegar, wine, salt, and tomatoes and cook for 2 minutes, stirring constantly. Add the remaining ingredients and cook for 4 more minutes. Remove from the heat and serve. Serves 6.

Lagniappe: This is a spicy, tempting treat. I like to eat this plain or over my Creamy "Mock" Potatoes or you can serve them over creamed turnips. This is also good over the low-carb noodle of your choice. You can make this dish completely in advance and either refrigerate or freeze for later use. To reheat, just thaw in the refrigerator and heat over low heat, stirring often until the chicken is heated through. It's a great recipe for a quick meal. A lot of people talk about buying the whole chicken and boning out the meat you want. I really find it much better to buy exactly what you are going to use. The only time I buy the whole chicken now is if I'm making stock or gumbos, or planning to use all the chicken to make a dish. Then it's worth it to get the whole chicken. Otherwise, buy what you need; it is cheaper in the long run. Not to mention the time saved!

Carbs per serving: 9.3 g.
Net carbs per serving: 7.9 g.
Calories per serving: 295

CHICKEN SPICY JACK

3 tbsp. unsalted butter

3 large cloves garlic, minced

1 shallot, minced

6 chicken breast halves, about 6 oz. each

1 tsp. Chicken Seasoning Mix (see p. 18)

½ cup dry white wine

1 tbsp. lime juice

½ cup red bell peppers, diced

2 cups Monterey Jack cheese, shredded

2 tbsp. fresh parsley, minced

Preheat the oven to 350 degrees. In a large non-stick skillet over medium-high heat, add the butter and let it melt and get hot. Add the garlic and shallots and sauté for 3 minutes. Season the chicken breasts with the Chicken Seasoning Mix and sauté for about 5 minutes on each side. When they are cooked, put them in a very lightly-greased, shallow baking dish. Add the wine and lime juice to the skillet and cook at high heat until the liquid is reduced by half. Add the bell pepper and cook over medium heat for 1 minute. Pour the liquid and the peppers on top of the chicken. Sprinkle evenly with the Monterey Jack cheese and the parsley. Bake uncovered for 15 minutes at 350 degrees. Remove and let sit for 3 minutes. Serve with lots of cheese sauce on top of each breast half. Serve hot. Serves 6.

Lagniappe: Not a difficult recipe, but it does have a few steps. You will be rewarded with the wonderful taste of the finished product. You can make this dish in advance, except for the baking. Refrigerate it until you are ready to bake. If you do, just bake for about 20 minutes at 325 degrees. Either way, this is a delightful dish.

Carbs per serving: 8.6 g.

Net Carbs per serving: 8.2 g.

Calories per serving: 534

SAUTÉED CHICKEN TENDERS

2 lb. boneless, skinless chicken strips

2 tsp. Chicken Seasoning Mix (see p. 18)

3 tbsp. extra virgin olive oil

2 tbsp. fresh basil, minced

4 cloves garlic, minced

2 jalapenos, seeds removed and minced

1 shallot, minced

1 tsp. Tabasco® Sauce

Season the chicken strips equally with the Chicken Seasoning Mix and set aside. In a heavy, large skillet over medium-high heat, add the olive oil and let the oil get hot. When the olive oil starts to smoke, brown the chicken tenders well for about 5 minutes on each side. When the chicken is cooked, add the basil, garlic, jalapenos, and shallots. Sauté for 5 minutes, stirring often. Add the Tabasco® Sauce and fresh parsley and stir well. Serve hot. Serves 6.

Lagniappe: This is a quick and easy recipe that lets you enjoy your chicken. It's better to eat the sautéed chicken without all the flour added that you usually get with chicken tenders. This is an all-meat version of a fast food dish that is loaded with carbs. Serve this with a nice salad and a side dish of your choice and you have a great meal. For variation, you can add a little wine at the end of the cooking process while the pan is very hot. You can deglaze the pan drippings, making a tangy light sauce.

Carbs per serving: 1.3 g.
Net carbs per serving: 1.1 g.
Calories per serving: 360

CHICKEN LASAGNA

Olive oil flavored baking spray
1½ lb. chicken breast, skinless
1½ tsp. Chicken Seasoning Mix (see p. 18)
3 tbsp. extra virgin olive oil
1½ cup onion, chopped
3 cloves garlic, minced
½ cup celery, minced
1 cup bell pepper, diced
1 cup fresh mushrooms, sliced
2 14.5-oz. cans tomatoes diced in sauce
1 cup of Chicken Stock (see p. 88) or chicken broth
½ cup dry Chianti
1 packet Splenda® sweetener
2 tsp. Italian seasoning

2 tsp. fresh basil, minced
½ tsp. oregano
½ cup black olives diced
¼ cup green stuffed olives, diced
8 large cabbage leaves
1 eggplant, peeled and sliced into ¼-inch thick slices the whole length of the eggplant
½ cup pepperoni slices
1 8-oz. container ricotta cheese
1 8-oz. container cream cheese, cut into 18 pieces
½ cup Parmesan cheese
¼ cup Romano cheese
1 cup Provolone cheese, grated
1 cup Mozzarella cheese, grated

Preheat the oven to 375 degrees. Spray the sides and bottom of a large lasagna pan (14 x 11 x 3) with olive oil flavored baking spray and set aside for later use. Season the chicken with the Chicken Seasoning Mix and bake it in a non-stick pan at 375 degrees for 35 minutes. When the chicken is cooked, remove it from the oven and chop it into bite-sized pieces; set it aside for later use. In a large, heavy skillet over medium-high heat, add the olive oil and sauté the onions, garlic, celery, and bell pepper for 7 minutes, stirring often. Add the mushrooms and sauté them for 1 minute, stirring constantly. Add the tomatoes and cook them over simmering heat for 10 minutes, stirring often. Add the Chicken Stock, Chianti, Splenda®, Italian seasoning, basil, oregano, and black and green olives. Sauté for 15 more minutes over a low simmering heat.

When you are ready to assemble, spread about ½ cup of the sauce on the bottom of the pan. Arrange 4 cabbage leaves so they cover the bottom of the pan and sit flat on the bottom. Arrange the following in the baking pan: ⅓ of the chopped chicken, ⅓ of the pepperoni, ⅓ of the ricotta cheese, ⅓ of the cream cheese, ⅓ of the Parmesan, and ⅓ of the

Romano cheese. Sprinkle ¼ of the Provolone and ¼ of the Mozzarella. Spoon about 1 cup of the sauce on top of the layer. Layer the slices of eggplant. It should take all the eggplant. Cover with the ⅓ layer of all the items as above and the ¼ cups of Provolone and Mozzarella. Spread out ½ cup of the sauce. Then spread the last 4 cabbage leaves on top of the eggplant layer. Layer the remaining third of the items as above and all the remaining sauce. Evenly spread all the remaining Provolone cheese and Mozzarella and sprinkle with the minced parsley. Bake for 1 hour at 375. When baked, remove from the oven and let the lasagna sit for 5 minutes then cut into 12 even pieces with a very sharp knife. Serve warm. Serves 12.

Lagniappe: This recipe takes a little time, but what results! The cabbage and eggplant help make this recipe feel and look like the real deal. With all that wonderful goodness, you'll wonder why you wanted to eat those egg noodles anyway! You can make it in advance and refrigerate or freeze leftovers with great success. This dish is good enough for company but still practical for everyday eating. You can substitute 2 lbs. of ground round for the chicken to make Low-Carb Lasagna. Change the seasoning to Beef Seasoning Mix, the stock to Beef Stock (see p. 86), add an extra teaspoon of the mix, then add the meat to the skillet, right after you sauté the vegetables. Sauté the ground round for 10 minutes, stirring constantly. Then proceed with the recipe as above, using beef for chicken each time. No matter which way you fix it, you've got a hit!

Carbs per serving: 10.4 g.
Net carbs per serving: 8.3 g.
Calories per serving: 361

CHICKEN ETOUFEE

½ cup peanut oil

2 tsp. Chicken Seasoning Mix (see p. 18)

13½-lb. fryer, cut into serving pieces

2 medium onions, chopped

1 medium red bell pepper, diced

¼ cup celery, minced

3 cloves garlic, minced

1 large tomato, skinned, seeds removed, and diced

½ cup green onions, chopped

2 tbsp. fresh parsley, minced

2 tsp. Tabasco® Sauce

Heat the oil in a large, heavy, deep skillet over medium-high heat until hot. Season the chicken equally with the seasoning mix, then add the chicken to the skillet and cook until browned evenly on all sides. Remove the pieces of chicken as they are browned. When all the chicken pieces are done, return them to the pot and reduce the heat to low. Cover the chicken with the vegetables and add the Tabasco® Sauce. Cover and cook the chicken over low heat for 1½ hours or until the chicken is tender and cooked through. Serve hot. Serves 6.

Lagniappe: While this dish is commonly served over white rice, you can just eat the chicken and the sauce with a fresh vegetable or a salad. This is genuine Cajun cooking at its best. This is the regular way to cook Etouffee; the only difference here is that we won't serve it over rice. You still have all the richness and goodness of the recipe to enjoy.

Carbs per serving: 4.8 g.
Net carbs per serving: 3.6 g.
Calories per serving: 764

CHICKEN FRICASEE

1 stewing hen, 4½ to 5 lb., cut into
    serving pieces
2 tsp. Chicken Seasoning Mix (see
    p. 18)
½ cup peanut oil
1 tbsp. whole wheat flour
2 tbsp. soy flour
2 medium onions, chopped
1 medium bell pepper, chopped

1 cup celery, chopped
3 cloves garlic, minced
10 large mushrooms, sliced
3 cups Chicken Stock (see p. 88) or
    chicken broth
½ cup green onion, tops only
2 tbsp. fresh parsley, minced
1 tsp. fresh basil, minced
2 tsp. Tabasco® Sauce

Season the chicken well with the Chicken Seasoning Mix. Put the peanut oil into a large, heavy saucepan that has a lid and heat it until the oil is hot over medium-high heat. Fry the chicken pieces a few at a time until nicely browned on all sides. Remove the chicken as it is browned to a large dish for holding until you are ready to use. Add the whole-wheat flour. Using a wire whisk, stir the flour until it becomes a dark brown. Never stop stirring. It should darken fast. When it has reached the desired color, add the soy flour, onions, bell pepper, celery, and garlic. Sauté for 5 minutes, then add the mushrooms and sauté for 2 more minutes. Return the chicken to the saucepan, add the Chicken Stock, stir well, cover, and cook for 2½ hours or until the chicken is tender, stirring occasionally. Just before it is time to serve add the green onions, fresh basil, parsley, and Tabasco® Sauce. Cook for 2 more minutes then serve. Serves 8.

Lagniappe: Fricassee is a dish that will satisfy the soul of any Cajun. It is easy, but it takes a little cooking time. You can serve it in a bowl with a spoon if you like, since you can't serve it over rice. The chicken is tender, juicy, and oh-so-tasty. You can make this dish completely in advance and refrigerate for later use. It will actually improve in the refrigerator. The flavors tend to intensify. When you are ready to serve, just reheat over low heat until the chicken pieces are hot. Talk about good eating!

Carbs per serving: 8.9 g.
Net carbs per serving: 7.4 g.
Calories per serving: 1064

POULET LE CHAMPIGNON

8 chicken breast halves, 6 oz. each

2 tbsp red wine vinegar

1 tbsp. balsamic vinegar

2 tbsp. extra virgin olive oil

2 tbsp. soy sauce

1 tsp. Tabasco® Sauce

5 cloves garlic, minced

1 tsp. salt

1 tsp. fresh ground black pepper

½ tsp. cayenne pepper

½ tsp. cloves, ground

1 tsp. hot dry mustard

1 packet Splenda® sweetener

2 tbsp. olive oil

1 onion, chopped

1 red bell pepper, cut into strips

1 pound mushrooms, sliced

1 cup broccoli flowerets

1 can sliced water chestnuts

¼ cup toasted pecans, chopped

1 tsp. red pepper flakes

Cut the chicken breasts into thin strips and set aside. In a large mixing bowl combine the next 12 ingredients, from the red wine vinegar through the Splenda®, and mix together well with a wire whisk. Put the chicken strips into the mixing bowl, cover with plastic wrap and refrigerate overnight or for 8 hours. When you are ready to cook, heat the olive oil in a large, heavy skillet over high heat. When the oil begins to pop, add the onions, red bell pepper, mushrooms, broccoli, water chestnuts, and pecans. Sauté for 3 minutes, stirring often. Then add the marinating chicken breasts and sauté for 7 minutes over high heat, stirring constantly. When the time is finished, add the pepper flakes and parsley and reduce the heat to simmer. Cover the skillet and cook over low heat for 15 more minutes, stirring a few times. Serve hot. Serves 6.

Lagniappe: This is a Cajun stir fry. It gives you the flavor of Cajun with the quickness of a stir fry. The quick cooking over high temperatures has a tendency to capture all the flavors of each ingredient and intensify them. This is a dish that should be eaten right after cooking. While it still tastes good after it has been refrigerated, the crispness of the vegetables and the texture of the mushroom change after the dish sits in the refrigerator. See note about balsamic vinegar on page 53.

Carbs per serving: 9.2 g.
Net carbs per serving: 5.9 g.
Calories per serving: 599

RUM LEGS

2 tbsp. soy sauce

2 tbsp. Worcestershire sauce

½ cup dark rum

1 tbsp. balsamic vinegar

2 tbsp. shallots, finely chopped

3 cloves garlic, finely minced

1 tsp. Tabasco® Sauce

1 tsp. ginger

1 tsp. sweet basil, minced

½ tsp. hot dry mustard

¼ tsp. ground cloves

¼ cup brown sugar Sweet and Low®

2 tbsp. parsley, finely minced

1½ lb. chicken legs

¼ cup dry red wine

Mix together all the ingredients except for the chicken in a large mixing bowl until well blended. In a non-stick baking dish, place all the legs one layer thick. Pour the mixed ingredients over the top of the chicken and cover tightly with plastic wrap. Marinate for 12 hours. Bake at 350 degrees for one hour, then remove the chicken from the pan to a warm serving platter. Place the baking pan over medium-high heat and deglaze the pan with the dry red wine, making sure to dissolve all the bits that stick to the bottom of the pan during baking. Let the wine reduce by about half and pour the reduced liquid over the chicken on the platter. Serve hot. Serves 6.

Lagniappe: This is a great way to serve chicken legs. It's spicy a little sweet at the same time. You can completely make it in advance and refrigerate until you are ready to serve. Just put the mixture back into a skillet and simmer until the chicken legs are hot. Although Splenda® is the only Atkins-approved sugar substitute, Sweet and Low® is the only company that makes a *brown* sugar substitute. As you can see, the carb count is still very low. See note about balsamic vinegar on page 53.

Carbs per serving: 4.6 g.
Net carbs per serving: 4.5 g.
Calories per serving: 311

CHICKEN QUESADILLAS

4 low-carb tortillas (3 net carbs each)
½ cup Pepper Jack cheese, grated
½ cup Colby cheese, grated
¼ cup Swiss cheese
1 green onion, chopped
¾ cup green bell pepper, julienned

¾ lb. grilled chicken breast, sliced thin
½ cup mushrooms, sliced
2 cloves garlic, minced
2 tbsp. extra virgin olive oil
¼ cup sour cream
spicy salsa to as desired

Place two tortillas each on a dinner plate. Spread half of the Pepper Jack cheese evenly on both tortillas. Repeat the process with the Colby cheese and then with the Swiss. Evenly spread the green onions and bell pepper on each of the two tortillas. Put half of the meat on each tortilla, spreading it out so that most of the tortilla is covered. Sprinkle evenly with the mushrooms and then the garlic. Cover evenly with the cheese then put the two unused tortillas on top of the cheese. In a medium skillet, add the olive oil and when it is hot one prepared Quesadilla onto the skillet, taking care not to spill out the insides. Heat over medium heat for 2 minutes, then using a spatula carefully turn it over. Cook, shaking the skillet gently for 2 more minutes, then flip it over and cook for 1 more minute. Transfer to a plate and keep it warm (165 to 170 degrees) while you repeat the entire process with the other tortillas, starting with the tablespoon of olive oil. When cooked serve with the sour cream and spicy salsa on the side.

Lagniappe: This is a great way to use leftover chicken from a barbecue or an evening grilling. You can vary the meat to fit your preference. I like to use thigh meat. You can also use ground chicken or chopped chicken, the kind you'd use in a chicken salad. Feel free to vary the cheeses to suit your taste. For that matter, you can vary any of the vegetables used as well.

Carbs per serving: 29.4 g.
Net carbs per serving: 12.6 g.
Calories per serving: 907

TURKEY CUTLETS AU WHITE ZINFANDEL

4 turkey cutlets, 7 oz. each
1 tsp. Cajun Seasoning Mix (see p. 20)
butter for greasing the dish
½ cup onions, finely chopped
¼ cup red bell pepper, diced
2 cloves garlic, finely minced
¼ cup celery, minced

1½ cups mushrooms, sliced
⅔ cup white Zinfandel wine
1 tbsp. fresh lemon juice
1 tsp. Tabasco® Sauce
½ tsp. fresh ground black pepper
2 tbsp. fresh parsley, minced
2 tbsp. extra virgin olive oil

Preheat the oven to 375 degrees. Season the turkey cutlets with the Cajun Seasoning Mix. Lightly butter the bottom and sides of a shallow, 2-quart baking dish. Place the turkey cutlets on the bottom of the dish. Cover them evenly with the vegetables. Combine the wine, lemon juice, and Tabasco® Sauce and pour the mixture over the cutlets. Sprinkle the black pepper and parsley over the cutlets, then drizzle the olive oil over the entire dish. Bake uncovered at 375 degrees for 45 minutes. Serve hot with plenty of sauce from the pan on the side. Serves 4.

Lagniappe: You can put this dish together for up to 2 days before cooking. Keep it tightly covered with plastic wrap and refrigerate until you are ready to cook. Do not cook the dish in advance. It needs to be eaten right after cooking. Turkey tends to get tough when it is refrigerated after cooking, especially when it is cooked in a liquid. The cooking is easy, so there is no need to cook it in advance. Just pop it in the oven 45 minutes before you need it.

Carbs per serving: 4.6 g.
Net carbs per serving: 4.2 g.
Calories per serving: 285

PAN FRIED CAJUN TURKEY

¼ cup peanut oil
4 turkey cutlets (about 8 oz. each
3 tsp. Cajun Seasoning Mix (see p. 20)

Heat a large, heavy skillet (black iron) over very high heat. Add the peanut oil. Season the turkey with the Cajun Seasoning Mix, taking care to push the seasoning into the cutlets with your fingers. When the peanut oil begins to smoke, carefully drop the cutlets one at a time into the skillet, giving the oil time to heat back up between each cutlet. Cook the cutlets about 1½ minutes on each side. Be sure to have your hood on full power, or better yet cook this outside because it makes a lot of smoke. Remove the cutlets from the skillet and quickly turn off the fire under the pot. Plate and serve. Serves 4.

Lagniappe: This is quick and so delicious. You won't believe the taste. You'll think you put too much seasoning, but a lot comes off in the cooking process. If you can't serve the turkey right away, cover with foil and keep in a 170-degree oven until you can serve. A nice salad and the Cajun Jack Cake (see p. 76) are good with this dish. The only problem with this dish is that you can't cook 8 or 10 of these without smoking up your house. So if you want to cook a bunch, you have to cook outside. Remember, you have to have the fire up all the way to sear the wonderful juices in and caramelize the seasoning mix. You'll want to serve this dish for company!

Carbs per serving: trace
Net carbs per serving: trace
Calories per serving: 326

Vegetables

GRILLED VEGETABLES

½ pound frozen broccoli spears, thawed

½ pound frozen cauliflower spears, thawed

1 large onion, quartered

¼ cup extra virgin olive oil

2 tsp. Seafood Seasoning Mix (see p. 17)

Heat the grill to hot. Rub the vegetables with the olive oil and season equally with the seasoning mix. Grill on a hot grill, turning when the grill marks begin to become dark brown, about 12 to 15 minutes. Serve immediately. Serves 6.

Lagniappe: This is simple and easy, but so good. The grill brings out the true flavor of the vegetables. While you can use fresh vegetables, frozen vegetables grill easier and in much less time. If you do use fresh vegetables, you will have to make sure the grill is not too hot or it will burn the outside of the vegetables before they are tender enough to eat.

Carbs per serving: 5.2 g
Net Carbs per serving: 3.5 g
Calories per serving: 102

CAULIFLOWER AU GRATIN

1 large head of cauliflower
1 slice Country White Atkins® bread
1 10 ¾-oz. can condensed cream of
    mushroom soup

½ cup half-and-half
¼ cup onions, finely chopped
1 cup Gouda cheese, shredded
paprika

Preheat the oven to 375 degrees. Wash and trip the cauliflower. In a large steamer, steam by turning on the heat and bringing the water in the steamer to a boil. Once the water starts to boil, turn off the heat and let the cauliflower stand in the steamer for 10 minutes. Take the bread and place it in a low oven. Let it toast and begin to dry out, about 15 minutes on low heat (about 225 degrees). Remove the bread and put into a food processor. Turn on and let the processor turn the bread to breadcrumbs. In a large saucepan over medium heat, add the mushroom soup, half-and-half, onions, and Gouda cheese. Stir until the cheese is melted and the sauce begins to bubble. Remove the cauliflower from the steamer and place in a casserole dish (about 2 quarts). Pour cheese sauce over the cauliflower. Sprinkle with the breadcrumbs, dust with paprika, and bake at 375 degrees for about 20 minutes. It should be golden brown. Serve hot. Serves 6 to 8.

Lagniappe: Don't let the length scare you; this is a very easy recipe. It just has a few extra steps that take a little time, but it isn't difficult. This can be used to make Broccoli au Gratin or Brussels Sprouts au Gratin by substituting broccoli or brussels sprouts into the recipe above.

Carbs per serving: 9.2 g.
Net Carbs per serving: 6.5 g.
Calories per serving: 205.3

Carbs per serving: 6.9 g.
Net Carbs per serving: 4.9 g.
Calories per serving: 154

CREAMY MOCK POTATOES

6 cups water
1 tsp. salt
1 head cauliflower, broken into pieces
¼ cup onions, chopped
2 cloves garlic, whole

2 tbsp. butter, lightly salted
½ tsp. salt
½ tsp. fresh ground black pepper
⅓ cup real mayonnaise
paprika to garnish

In a large heavy pot over high heat, bring the water and salt to a hard boil. When the water is at a hard, rolling boil, add the cauliflower pieces, onion, and garlic. Stir the vegetables through the boiling water, cover, and let boil for 5 minutes. Turn the heat down to simmer and cook for 7 more minutes. Remove from the heat and pour the cauliflower, onion, and garlic into a colander to drain. Once drained, place all three ingredients into a food processor and process at full power for 3 minutes. Add the butter, salt, and pepper and continue to blend until the cauliflower is whipped to a nice white fluffy texture, about 5 to 7 more minutes as full power. You can pulse a few times to make sure all of the vegetables are completely blended. Add the mayonnaise and blend it through completely. Pour into a serving bowl land dust very lightly with paprika. Serve immediately. Serves 6.

Lagniappe: I know what you are saying. If you can't have mashed potatoes, then you really don't want to eat fake potatoes! But try it—it will surprise you. It is very, very hard to tell the difference. I had my daughter, Christine, eat it believing it was mashed potatoes. Her only comment was it was a little too rich for her. Now let me quickly say, she doesn't like cauliflower! So for her to eat it was a major challenge, but for her to think it was mashed potatoes was phenomenal. You just have to give it a try. Serve as you would any mashed potatoes.

Carbs per serving: 5.2 g.
Net carbs per serving: 3.1 g.
Calories per serving: 149

MOCK LOADED BAKED POTATO

6 au gratin dishes
1 recipe Creamy Mock Potatoes (see p. 239)
butter flavored oil spray

1 cup of sharp cheddar cheese, shredded
½ cup green onions, minced
¾ cup sour cream
fresh ground black pepper for garnish

Preheat the oven to broil. Using a large spatula, spread the mock potatoes on the bottom and around the sides of each dish. You should use about ⅔ of the mixture. Put into the broiler and let the potatoes cook for about 3 minutes, about 6 inches away from the heat, to brown nicely. Remove from the oven and set aside. Reduce the heat to 425 degrees. Mix the cheddar, green onions, and ½ of the sour cream into the remaining potato mixture. Using the spatula, divide the potato/cheese mixture equally into each of the au gratin dishes. Put the dishes back into the hot oven and let the dish cook for 4 minutes; the cheese should melt. Remove from the oven and spoon the remaining sour cream equally onto each "baked potato." Garnish with black pepper and minced chives. Serve hot. Serves 6.

Lagniappe: Who says you can't have a baked potato on a low-carb diet? This will win over all those who say they can't do without baked potatoes! This is a great alternative. You'll think you've died and gone to Carb Heaven! To cut on the time, you can do everything in advance up to the baking. Just bake at 375 for 6 minutes and follow the recipe as above. Keep the "potato" in the refrigerator until you are ready to proceed. It will keep for up to 12 hours and still have great texture.

Carbs per serving: 7.9 g.
Net carbs per serving: 5.5 g.
Calories per serving: 366

CELERY BAYOU VISTA

8 stalks celery, cut on the diagonal into ½-inch pieces

1 tsp. salt

1 tsp. Tabasco® Sauce

¼ cup unsalted butter

1 cup onions, chopped

1 cup pecans, chopped

1 tsp. fine lemon zest

1 tsp. Splenda® sweetener

In a large pot, add the celery, salt, and Tabasco® Sauce and bring to a boil. Cook until tender, but still crisp, about 5 minutes. Remove from the heat and drain well. In a large skillet over medium-high heat, add the butter and let it melt and get hot. Sauté the onions, pecans, and lemon zest for 5 more minutes. Add the Splenda® and stir it well. Serve hot. Serves 6.

Lagniappe: This is a great side dish. Celery is usually just a seasoning added to other vegetables or main dishes, but this dish puts the celery center stage. The crunchiness of the celery and the pecans bring this dish together. It's easy and surprisingly good.

Carbs per serving: 4.8 g.
Net Carbs per serving: 3.7 g.
Calories per serving: 210

RUTABAGA À LA CAJUN

2 cups rutabaga, cut into ½-inch pieces
water to cover
1 tsp. salt
3 tbsp. unsalted butter

½ cup onions, chopped
1 clove garlic, minced
1 tbsp. fresh parsley, finely minced
1 tsp. Tabasco® Sauce

Put the rutabaga in a medium pot, cover with the water, and add the salt. Bring to a boil, then lower the heat to a simmering low boil. Let the rutabaga cook for 15 minutes. Remove from the heat and drain. While the rutabaga is cooling, in a medium sized heavy skillet over medium heat, add the butter and let it get hot. Add the onions and garlic. Sauté for 3 minutes, then add the rutabaga, parsley, and Tabasco® Sauce. Sauté for 4 more minutes, stirring often. Serve immediately. Serves 6.

Lagniappe: Rutabaga is a wonderful tasting vegetable that so very often goes unused by the general public. Most people really don't know what to do with it. It's easy to cook and has such a unique flavor that it can carry itself as a side dish. Try serving this to company and you'll have them begging for the recipe.

Carbs per serving: 6.4 g.
Net Carbs per serving: 5.1 g.
Calories per serving: 79.2

FRIED CABBAGE

5 cups cabbage, shredded

2 cups onions, chopped

1 cup celery, sliced thin

1 cup bell pepper, diced

2 cups fresh tomatoes, skinned, seeded and diced

¼ cup bacon fat

2 packets Splenda® sweetener

1 tsp. salt

1 tsp. fresh ground black pepper

1 tsp. Tabasco® Sauce

½ tsp. fresh basil, minced

In a large heavy skillet over medium-high heat, add all the ingredients, cover, and let stand for 3 minutes. Remove the cover and stir well, making sure that anything that stuck to the pan is stirred loose. Put the cover back on and let it cook for 3 more minutes, stir well and repeat the process again for another 3 minutes. Remove the lid for the final time and stir well. Serve hot. Serves 6.

Lagniappe: This makes a wonderful cabbage stew. It's easy and the taste is great. You can make this dish in advance; just cook it for 6 minutes and remove from the heat and refrigerate. When you are ready to serve, put the skillet on medium-high heat and, stirring often, cook the cabbage until it is hot, about 5 minutes.

Carbs per serving: 8.7 g.

Net carbs per serving: 6.3 g.

Calories per serving: 97

SMOTHERED CABBAGE WITH CHEESE

5 cups cabbage, shredded
½ cup water
1 tsp. Tabasco® Sauce
1 tsp. salt

1 tsp. fresh ground black pepper
½ cup onions, chopped
¾ cup sharp Cheddar cheese, grated

In a large saucepot add all the ingredients except for the cheese. Bring to a boil over high heat, then reduce to a low rolling boil and cook covered for 10 minutes. Remove from the heat and drain well. Add the cheese and put back on low heat and cook for 2 minutes, stirring constantly. Serve immediately. Serves 6.

Lagniappe: A wonderful dish for those who like cabbage. You can make this dish in advance and refrigerate until you are ready to serve. Cooked cabbage seems to get better once it has set for a while. When you are ready to serve, just heat over low heat, stirring often until it is hot. I also like to eat this cold, right from the fridge. It's got such a great flavor.

Carbs per serving: 4.5 g.
Net Carbs per serving: 3 g.
Calories per serving: 77

MUSHROOMS BATON ROUGE

¼ cup unsalted butter

1 pound mushrooms, sliced

1 bunch green onions

2 cloves garlic, finely minced

1 tsp. Beef Seasoning Mix (see p. 19)

1 tbsp. fresh parsley, finely minced

In a large skillet over medium-high heat, melt the butter and let it get hot. Add the mushrooms and sauté for 3 minutes. While the mushrooms are sautéing, cut the green onions in pieces about 3-inches long, then slice them lengthwise. Add the garlic, seasoning, and parsley and sauté for 5 more minutes. Serve immediately. Serves 6.

Lagniappe: This is a good side dish. I also like to use it to top grilled steak, chicken breast, or grilled fish. The flavor blends well with almost any meat dish. Any leftovers can be refrigerated and reheated at a later date. They will store in the refrigerator for up to 5 days if you tightly cover them. A great addition to any meal.

Carbs per serving: 6.1 g.

Net Carbs per serving: 4.3 g.

Calories per serving: 97

LIMAS MANUEL

1 10-oz. package frozen lima beans,
    thawed
¼ cup onions, chopped
2 cloves garlic, minced

1 tsp. Seafood Seasoning Mix (see
    p. 17)
1 tsp. Tabasco® Sauce
1 cup sour cream

Preheat the oven to 375 degrees. Place all the ingredients in a baking dish. Stir well and bake covered for 35 minutes at 375 degrees. Remove and let stand for 3 minutes, then serve. Serves 4.

Lagniappe: This is the dish for those who like limas. It's easy and the taste will blow you away. How can something so easy taste so good? It's all that sour cream! You can bake and refrigerate if you like, but it's so easy you shouldn't have to do anything in advance. While this is a little high even in net carbs, it is good to eat beans every once and a while. This is easy and tasty. Enjoy!

Carbs per serving: 25.8 g.
Net Carbs per serving: 18.4
Calories per serving: 248

FAUX BAKED BEANS

4 cups cauliflower, cut into flowerets
water to cover
1 tsp. salt
1 lb. ground meat
1 tsp. Beef Seasoning Mix (see p. 19)
1 cup onions, chopped
½ cup bell peppers, diced
¼ cup celery, chopped
2 cloves garlic, minced
1 tsp. Tabasco® Sauce

1 cup Low-Carb Homemade Catsup
(see p. 41) or low-carb catsup
½ cup Monterey Pepper Jack cheese,
shredded
½ cup medium cheddar cheese,
shredded
¼ cup half-and-half cream
¼ tsp. sharp cheddar cheese, grated
¼ cup parsley, fresh minced

In a large, heavy pot over medium-high heat, add the cauliflower and cover with water. Bring it to a hard boil. When it starts to boil, turn the heat down to simmer and cook for 5 minutes. Remove from the heat and let the cauliflower stand for 3 minutes in the water, then completely drain and set aside for later use. In a large skillet, over medium-high heat, add the ground meat, onions, bell pepper, celery, and garlic. Sauté for 7 minutes, stirring often. The meat should be browned. Preheat the oven to 350 degrees. Add the catsup and Tabasco® Sauce and blend into the meat well. Continue to cook for 3 more minutes. Take the drained cauliflower and cut it into small pieces and fold it into the meat sauce. Stir in well. Remove the skillet from the heat and stir in the cheeses and half-and-half. Pour into a lightly greased baking dish. Cover with the sharp cheddar and minced parsley and bake at 350 degrees for 35 minutes. Serve hot. Serves 8.

Lagniappe: While this isn't quite as close to the real thing as cauliflower mashed potatoes, this is quite an interesting faux bean recipe. It is close enough to a bean taste that you'll convince many at the table that you are serving beans. Of course, the carb count is significantly less. You can completely make this in advance and refrigerate until you are ready to serve. Just defrost and bake as above. A great side dish!

Carbs per serving: 9.2 g.
Net carbs per serving: 6.7 g.
Calories per serving: 370

EASY SMOTHERED OKRA

2 lb. fresh okra, tender
1 cup onions, chopped
¼ cup celery, chopped
¼ cup bell pepper, chopped
2 cloves garlic, minced
1 large fresh tomato, diced

2 tsp. Seafood Seasoning Mix (see p. 17)
1 tsp. Tabasco® Sauce
½ tsp. fresh sweet basil, minced
3 tbsp. peanut oil

Preheat the oven to 375 degrees. Put all the ingredients in a heavy, metal pot that has a lid and stir together well. Cover and place in a 375-degree oven for 45 minutes. Remove from the oven, carefully remove the cover, and stir well. Recover and return to the oven and bake for 20 more minutes. Remove and serve. Serves 8.

Lagniappe: The first time you cook this you'll say it won't work. When you normally cook okra you have to stir and stir. Then you have to deal with all that slime. Well, none of that. Cooking in the oven does it for you. You can cook in advance and refrigerate until you are ready to serve. You can reheat either on top of the stove or in a microwave. It's the only way to cook okra!

Carbs per serving: 11.1 g.
Net carbs per serving: 7.6 g.
Calories per serving: 95

SQUASH MARIE

3 tbsp. extra virgin olive oil
3 tbsp. shallots, minced
3 cloves garlic, minced
2 tsp. Seafood Seasoning Mix (see p. 17)
2 lb. yellow squash, cut about ½-inch thick

2 large tomatoes, diced
¼ cup fresh basil, finely chopped
1½ cups Parmesan cheese, grated
½ cup Romano cheese, grated
¼ cup fresh parsley, minced

In a large, heavy skillet over medium-high heat, add the olive oil and heat until it gets hot and starts to pop. Sauté the shallots and garlic for 3 minutes, stirring often. Season the squash with the seasoning mix, then add it to the sauté and cook for 8 minutes, stirring often. Add the tomato and basil and cook for 2 minutes. Add the cheeses and fresh parsley. Stir well, then heat for 1 minute. Serve hot. Serves 8.

Lagniappe: This is a dish for those who like squash! The flavor of squash blends well with the tomato and basil. This dish can be refrigerated and reheated for later use. Squash is such a nice, fresh vegetable to cook and the bright yellow color adds eye appeal to almost any dish. Enjoy!

Carbs per serving: 6.6 g.
Net carbs per serving: 6.1 g.
Calories per serving: 437

SQUASH CASSEROLE LANNETTE

2 tbsp. extra virgin olive oil
1 cup onions, finely chopped
2 cloves garlic, minced
2 tbsp. celery, minced
½ cup banana peppers, mild and multicolored, diced
1½ lb. yellow squash, tender and young

1 tsp. Seafood Seasoning Mix (see p. 17)
1 large egg, beaten
1 cup sour cream
½ cup colby cheese

Preheat the oven to 350 degrees. In a large, heavy skillet over medium-high heat, add the olive oil and let it get hot. When the oil is hot, add the onions, garlic, celery, and banana peppers. Sauté for 5 minutes. In a large mixing bowl, add the squash, sautéed vegetables, and the remaining ingredients. stir together well, then pour into a lightly-greased, 10 x 10 baking dish and bake at 350 degrees for 30 minutes. Serve immediately. Serves 6.

Lagniappe: This is a tasty casserole that highlights the squash. It is light and makes a wonderful side dish for any meat dish you might serve. It can be put together in advance and stored in the refrigerator ready to bake, or you can completely bake it and reheat it. It is a wonderful dish to bring to a buffet and a great way to use fresh squash.

Carbs per serving: 7.9 g.
Net carbs per serving: 6 g.
Calories per serving: 239

PAN-FRIED BROCCOLI GRATE

2 cups broccoli stems, grated

3 eggs, separated

1 tsp. Tabasco® Sauce

1 tbsp. soy flour

¼ cup Swiss cheese

1 tsp. Seafood Seasoning Mix (see p. 17)

3 tbsp. unsalted butter

Add the broccoli to a large bowl and set aside. Divide the eggs into two small bowls. with a wire whisk, whip the egg whites until they are stiff. Whip the egg yolks with the Tabasco® Sauce and soy flour until it thickens a bit. Add the cheese to the yolk mixture and season with the seasoning mix. Fold this yolk mixture into the grated broccoli and carefully fold in the egg whites. In a large heavy skillet over medium-high heat, add the butter. When the butter is melted and hot, drop the broccoli by heaping tablespoons onto the skillet and cook until the patty has set. Flip them over carefully and fry the other side until they are golden brown. Transfer to a serving platter and repeat the process until all the batter is used. Serve warm. Serves 6.

Lagniappe: This is a different way to serve vegetables! To grate the broccoli, trim the big stems from the broccoli heads and grate them with a vegetable grater as you would grate carrots. The flavor of broccoli is quite strong in the stems and it very often is the part of the broccoli that you toss. I learned to cook this when I was a chef at Old Vienna Restaurant. I had a number of Chinese waiters who told me that Americans throw away the best part of vegetables. Ever since, I've tried to use as much of the vegetable as I can. This is a great side dish or a wonderful snack.

Carbs per serving: 2.3 g.
Net carbs per serving: 1.6 g.
Calories per serving: 159

TURNIPS GASTON

5 medium turnips
water to cover turnips
1 tsp. salt for water
3 tbsp. unsalted butter
½ cup onions, chopped

2 tbsp. celery, minced
1 tsp. Seafood Seasoning Mix (see
  p. 17)
1 tsp. Tabasco® Sauce

Wash the turnips and trim them so the root and top are cut off. In a large pot, cover the turnips with salted water and boil for 15 minutes over high heat. Remove from the heat and let them sit in the salted water for 10 minutes. Remove the turnips, let them cool, and slice them about ¼-inch thick. In a large skillet over medium-high heat, add the butter and let it melt and get hot. Add the onions and celery and sauté for 3 minutes, stirring constantly. Add the turnips, seasoning mix, and Tabasco® Sauce and stir well and let the turnips sauté for 8 minutes, taking care to sauté both sides. Serve hot. Serves 6.

Lagniappe: This is the way to serve turnips if you either really love turnips or you've planted them and have to find a way to use as many as you can. This is almost just turnips. I really love this dish when the turnips just come in and are young, tender, and sweet. As the turnips get older, they have a much stronger flavor and are not nearly as tender. You can also add cooked ground meat or sausage make a wonderful main dish.

Carbs per serving: 5.9 g.
Net carbs per serving: 3.7 g.
Calories per serving: 80

PAN-FRIED TOMATOES

1 tbsp. extra virgin olive oil
½ tbsp. unsalted butter
4 cups cherry tomatoes, washed
2 tsp. fresh basil, minced

1 tsp. Seafood Seasoning Mix (see
  p. 17)
½ tsp. fresh rosemary, chopped
3 tbsp. Parmesan cheese

In a large heavy skillet over medium-high heat, add the oil and butter and let the butter melt and get hot. Add the remaining ingredients, except for the cheese. Sauté, gently stirring the pan until the tomatoes are hot and the skin starts to crack. Reduce the heat and sauté over low heat for 3 more minutes. Sprinkle with the Parmesan cheese and serve hot. Serves 6.

Lagniappe: Sometimes simple recipes taste great. This is one of those recipes, especially with the new varieties of super flavorful cherry tomatoes. You should serve this recipe immediately after cooking. The quality of the tomatoes falls apart if you try to reheat the dish. But don't worry; it's already quick and easy.

Carbs per serving: 5.4 g.
Net carbs per serving: 4.1 g.
Calories per serving: 81

OVEN-BAKED TOMATOES

4 medium tomatoes, ripe
¼ cup unsalted butter
½ cup onions, minced
2 cloves garlic, minced
2 tbsp. celery, finely minced

1 tbsp. Creole mustard
1 tbsp. white wine
1 tsp. Tabasco® Sauce
1 tsp. Worcestershire Sauce
1 cup crushed pork skins

Preheat the oven to 350 degrees. Cut the tomatoes in half and arrange on a lightly-greased baking sheet. Do not let the tomatoes touch each other. In a small skillet over medium-high heat, add the butter. When the butter is hot, add the onions, garlic, and celery and sauté for 5 minutes, stirring constantly. Add all the remaining ingredients except for the pork skins and cheese. Blend in well and spoon the seasoned butter on top of each tomato half. Mix together the pork skins and Romano cheese until well blended. Cover with an equal amount of crushed pork skins and cheese mixture and bake for 25 minutes at 350 degrees. Serve hot. Serves 8.

Lagniappe: Hot tomatoes are a nice side dish to almost any meal. It adds such color and flavor to the plate. You can completely prepare this dish for baking and set aside in the refrigerator until you are ready. This should be eaten right after you cook it. It does not refrigerate well. The texture falls apart. The best way to crush pork skins is to put them in a food processor and pulse until they are reduced to crumbs. Or you can do it the old fashioned way. Place the skins on wax paper, fold the paper over the pork, cover with a dishtowel, and beat gently with a rolling pin, or simply roll the pin over the skins. The method I use depends on how much hostility I need to relieve!

Carbs per serving: 4.4 g.
Net carbs per serving: 3.4 g.
Calories per serving: 134

Desserts

BLUEBERRY DELIGHT

1½ cups fresh blueberries
1 8-oz. package cream cheese
1 small lemon, juice only

½ cup Splenda® sweetener
¾ 8-oz. container Cool Whip®, to top
dish

Wash the blueberries well and let them dry. In a food processor, blend the cream cheese, lemon juice, and Splenda® at high speed until it is smooth and creamy. Add the Cool Whip® and blend at high speed until it is completely mixed. Add about 15 blueberries to the food processor and blend for 1 minute. Spoon out the mixture into a glass dish or into a nice sherbet glass. Place a handful of berries on the cream filling. Cover tightly with plastic wrap and let the mixture refrigerate for 2 hours. Remove the plastic wrap and top with about 1 tbsp. fresh whipped cream. Serve immediately. Serves 8.

Lagniappe: You won't believe this is a low-carb dessert. In fact, you will wonder why you would ever serve this any other way. With fresh blueberries and a rich cream filling, you'd think you were eating the finest cheesecake. For a slight change of pace, try lime juice instead of the lemon; you get a wonderful taste shift with basically the same recipe.

Carbs per serving: 11g.
Net Carbs per serving: 10.2g.
Calories per serving: 187

DREAMY STRAWBERRIES

1 8-oz. package cream cheese
1 small lemon, juice only
1 tsp. fresh lemon zest
½ cup Splenda® sweetener

1½ cups fresh strawberries, cut in thirds
1 tsp. vanilla extract
¾ 8-oz. container Cool Whip®, to top dish

In a food processor, add the cream cheese, lemon juice, zest, and Splenda® and blend at high speed until it is smooth and creamy. Add the Cool Whip® and blend at high speed until it is completely mixed. Add about 5 strawberries and the vanilla and blend for 1 minute. Spoon out the mixture into a glass dish or into a nice sherbet glass. Place a handful of berry slices on the cream filling. Cover tightly with plastic wrap and let the mixture refrigerate for 2 hours. Remove the plastic wrap and top with about 1 tbsp. fresh whipped cream. Serve immediately. Serves 8.

Lagniappe: Select rich red strawberries for the most tempting treat. You are better served if you pick strawberries that are in season in your area. They generally are picked at the peak of flavor.

Carbs per serving: 9.1 g.
Net Carbs per serving: 8.4 g.
Calories per serving: 180

FRESH CHERRY CREAM SURPRISE

1½ cups fresh cherries
1 8-oz. package cream cheese
1 small lemon, juice only
2 tsp. fresh lemon zest

½ cup Splenda® sweetener
1½ tsp. vanilla extract
¾ 8-oz. container Cool Whip®, to top dish

Wash the cherries well. Using a sharp paring knife, cut them in half and remove the pit and discard it. In a food processor, add the cream cheese, lemon juice, zest, and Splenda® and blend at high speed until it is smooth and creamy. Add the Cool Whip® and blend at high speed until it is completely mixed. Add about 10 whole cherries and the vanilla extract to the food processor and blend for 1 minute more. Spoon out the mixture into a glass dessert dish or into a nice champagne glass. Place a handful of cherry halves on the cream mixture. Cover tightly with plastic wrap and let the mixture refrigerate for 2 hours. Remove the plastic wrap and top with about 1 tbsp. fresh whipped cream. Serve immediately. Serves 8.

Lagniappe: This is easy, delicious, and quick to make and serve. It's perfect for when cherries are in season. For variety you can use the dark red cherries or the golden ones, as long as they are fresh. Fresh cherries are such a treat and using them makes your meal special. Be sure to select sweet cherries rather than the tart, sour ones. Sweet cherries are almost a dessert by themselves!

Carbs per serving: 10.7 g.
Net Carbs per serving: 10.2 g.
Calories per serving: 188

CLASSIC NEW YORK-STYLE CHEESECAKE

1½ cup pecan pieces

3 packets Splenda®

2 tbsp. soy flour

3 tbsp. unsalted butter

4 8-oz. packages cream cheese, softened

¼ tbsp. soy flour

4 egg yolks

3 whole eggs

1 cup Splenda®

1 tbsp. vanilla

1 cup sour cream

Preheat the oven to 325 degrees. Put the pecan pieces, 3 packets Splenda®, 2 tbsp. soy flour, and butter in a food processor and blend until well mixed. Pat the mixture into a 9-inch, non-stick, spring form pan. Bake for 10 minutes at 325 degrees then set aside for later use. In a large mixing bowl add the cream cheese, remaining soy flour, egg yolks and whole eggs, Splenda®, and vanilla. Beat with an electric mixer until well blended, then add the sour cream and blend again until the sour cream is completely mixed. Pour into the prepared spring form pan over the pecan crust. Bake for 1 hour and 15 minutes. The center of the cake should be set. Check by sticking a toothpick into the center of the cake; if it comes out clean, the cake is ready. If it does not, continue to bake for 5 more minutes and check again. Let the cake cool before you remove the spring-form rim. You can use a sharp knife around the edges to make sure the cake comes off the pan clean. Refrigerate for 6 hours or overnight before serving. Serves 15.

Lagniappe: This is a wonderful cheesecake. You won't be able to tell much difference between this and the higher carb version. I like to serve it with fresh berries on top or on the side. This cake will keep for up to 1 week refrigerated, if you can keep people from sneaking it out of the fridge. I like fresh raspberries, blueberries, or strawberries with the cake. They compliment it well.

Carbs per serving: 5.9 g.
Net Carbs per serving: 5.2 g.
Calories per serving: 344

CHOCOLATE MOUSSE

1 8-oz. package cream cheese, softened
½ cup Splenda® sweetener
2 1-oz. squares unsweetened baking chocolate

3 egg yolks, beaten
½ cup half-and-half
1 tsp. vanilla extract
1 8-oz. container Cool Whip®

In a food processor, blend the cream cheese until it is soft and beaten. Mix together the egg yolks and the half-and-half in a heavy pot or the top of a double boiler. Add the vanilla and stir well. Cook the egg yolk mixture until it begins to thicken, stirring constantly. Set aside for later use. Melt the chocolate in a microwave, about 1½ minutes. Pour a little of the egg mixture into the melted chocolate and blend together until mixed. Then add the remaining egg mixture to the chocolate and blend together well. Pour the chocolate egg mixture into the whipped cream cheese and blend until the egg mixture is completely blended, scraping the sides a few times to make sure that all the cream cheese mixture is blended. Add the Cool Whip® and blend until all the egg mixture is blended. Spoon the mixture into 8 small bowls, cover tightly, and chill for at least 4 hours. Serve chilled. Serves 8.

Lagniappe: What a great dessert! It's hard to find any diet that allows dessert, but on a low-carb diet, you don't have to say no to chocolate. I like to top it with whipped cream to add a little something special to the dessert. You can also put your favorite nuts, like pecans or walnuts, right into the dessert. Just blend with the rest as soon as you put the cream cheese into the dish. It tastes wonderful.

Carbs per serving 10.7 g.
Net carbs per serving: 10.2 g.
Calories per serving 277

EASY GRAND MARNIER® MOUSSE

3 oz. sugar-free white chocolate
1 tbsp. Grand Marnier® liqueur
2 tbsp. water
5 egg yolks

2 egg whites
¼ cup Splenda® sweetener
1 cup heavy whipping cream
1 tsp. orange zest

Put the white chocolate, Grand Marnier®, and water into a small pan over low heat and cook, stirring often until the white chocolate is melted. Remove from the heat and slowly beat in the 5 egg yolks until they are completely blended. Return to the very low heat and cook for 2 minutes, stirring constantly. Remove from the heat and set aside for later use. Put the two egg whites into a blender and beat until they are foamy; add ½ of the Splenda® sweetener and blend until mixed in. Add the whipping cream to the blender with the remaining sweetener and blend until the cream whips up. Slowly add the egg/chocolate mixture to the blender a little at a time until all is mixed well. Pour into individual ramekins and sprinkle with a little orange zest. Refrigerate until the mousse becomes firm. Serve chilled. Serves 6.

Lagniappe: This is a takeoff on the original Grand Marnier® Mousse, but this version is easy and has significantly fewer carbs. You can find sugar-free white chocolate in most baking sections. You can also use sugar-free white chocolate bars found in the sugar-free candy section. The products that are available today really make eating low-carb much easier, especially if you have a sweet tooth. I couldn't find a carb-free Grand Marnier®, but 1 tbsp. spread over 6 servings gives the orange taste without all the carbs. This is a special dessert!

Carbs per serving: 11.4 g.
Net carbs per serving: 2.3 g.
Calories per serving: 272

BRANDIED EGGNOG MOUSSE

1 .3-oz. packet lemon sugar-free
  gelatin
½ cup boiling water
¼ cup brandy
3 egg yolks, beaten
½ cup half-and-half

¼ cup Splenda® sweetener
2 egg whites,
1 cup heavy whipping cream
2 tbsp. Splenda® sweetener
1 tsp. vanilla extract
1 tsp. fresh lemon zest

Place the packet of gelatin into a medium-sized metal mixing bowl. Pour the boiling water on top of the gelatin and stir until it is dissolved. Add the brandy and half-and-half and mix in well. Add the well-beaten egg yolks a little at a time and whip in with a wire whisk until all the egg yolks are used. Place the metal bowl on top of a small pot with water in it and bring the water to a boil. Hold on to the metal bowl with your fingers and beat the egg mixture as the bowl heats up. Don't let the bowl stay on the boiling water longer than you can take the temperature of the bowl on your fingers. As the bowl gets a little too warm, lift it off the heat, but continue to whip with the whisk. Continue this process for 4 minutes. The liquid should become somewhat thickened. Remove from the heat and whip for one minute. Place the mixture in the refrigerator. While the gelatin/egg yolk mixture is refrigerating, beat the two egg whites with the ¼ cup of Splenda® until stiff peaks form. Then, with cool blades on your mixer, whip the whipping cream with the remaining Splenda® and vanilla until it becomes stiff as well. Fold in the egg whites into the cool gelatin mixture until well mixed. Now fold in the whipped cream taking care not to over stir, but make sure it is well blended. Pour into 8 individual soufflé dishes and refrigerate until it is congealed, about 3 hours. Garnish with lemon zest. Serves 8.

Lagniappe: What a dessert! It takes a little work, but this dessert will knock the socks off your guests. They will not believe that it's low carb! This is company dinner dessert. It's great during the holiday season, but also super any time of year. During the holidays, I like to add ½ teaspoon of nutmeg to the dish, along with the vanilla extract. You can also use a bit of green sugar to help decorate. Don't limit yourself to just the holiday season to serve this wonderful dessert.

Carbs per serving: 2.8 g.
Net carbs per serving: 2.8 g.
Calories per serving: 202

FRESH BLUEBERRY ICE CREAM

3 8-oz. packages fresh blueberries
2 tbsp. Equal® sweetener
1 tbsp. Splenda® sweetener

1 cup heavy whipping cream
1 tsp. fresh lemon juice

Wash and pick any stems from the blueberries. Return to their containers and put in the freezer until the berries are quite hard. Place in a food processor with a metal blade and process by pulsing on and off until the berries are all chopped. Add the Equal® and Splenda® and pulse again until the sweetener is mixed in well. With the processor running, drizzle the cream and lemon juice into the berries until all is used. Pour into a glass bowl and tightly cover with plastic wrap and return to the freezer. Let freeze for 20 minutes, then scoop and serve. Serves 8.

Lagniappe: This is a quick "ice cream" that is low in carbs, high in taste, and easy to make. It is not the kind of ice cream that you can store for a long time, but it's a quick treat to serve as an great ending to a good meal. You can keep the blueberries frozen until you are ready to make this dessert. You can also serve it without refreezing if you like; it just will not be quite as firm. You can also make wonderful Fresh Peach Ice Cream or Fresh Apricot Ice Cream by substituting peeled peach slices or peeled apricot slices for the blueberries and following the recipe as above. Both are great desserts.

Carbs per serving: 9 g.
Net Carbs per serving: 7.5 g.
Calories per serving: 186

FROZEN LIME SOUFFLÈ

3 limes
6 egg whites
¼ cup Splenda® sweetener

1½ cup heavy whipping cream
¼ cup Splenda® sweetener
1 drop green food color

Using a lemon zester remove most of the lime zest from the 3 limes and set aside for later use. Juice the limes until you get most of the lime juice from them and set the juice aside. In a large bowl, beat the egg whites and ¼ cup of Splenda® until they start to get stiff. Add ¼ tsp. of lime zest and ½ of the lime juice to the egg whites. In another bowl, beat the heavy cream until it starts to get stiff, then add the remaining Splenda®, lime juice, ¼ tsp. lime zest, and the green food color and continue to beat until the whipped cream is stiff. Fold the egg white mixture into the whipped cream mixture and pour into 10 individual soufflé cups. Sprinkle with the remaining lime zest, cover tightly with plastic wrap, and freeze for 3 or 4 hours. Serve frozen. Serves 10.

Lagniappe: A wonderful dessert! Sometimes I put just a dab of whipped cream on top of each soufflé and sprinkle with a little more lime zest and serve. This is a light, yet tasty, dessert. You can make it up to 3 days in advance. Just remember to keep it tightly covered with the plastic wrap in the freezer until you are ready to serve. Then remove from the freezer, decorate, and serve. Even though it is frozen, it will have the consistency of soft ice cream and is easy to eat. You can use the same recipe and substitute orange juice and orange zest to make Frozen Orange Soufflé. Just remember that you'll use 3 small naval oranges and your carb count will be a little bit higher using orange juice instead of lime juice, but it's still a nice treat!

Carbs per serving: 3.5 g.
Net carbs per serving: 3.5 g.
Calories per serving: 150

INDIVIDUAL STRAWBERRY CHEESECAKES

2½ cups fresh strawberries, sliced
2 tbsp. Splenda® sweetener
¼ tsp. ginger
½ tsp. fresh grated orange zest, finely grated
3 8-oz. packages cream cheese, softened

½ cup Splenda® sweetener
2 tbsp. fresh lemon juice
½ tsp. fresh grated lemon zest, finely grated
1 tsp. vanilla
1 large egg, lightly beaten

Preheat the oven to 325 degrees. Grease an 18-hole (1½ to 2-inch size) muffin pan and set aside. In a small mixing bowl, add the strawberries, 3 tbsp. Splenda®, ginger, and orange zest and let it stand until you are ready to use. Combine in a large mixing bowl the cream cheese, ½ cup Splenda®, lemon juice, lemon zest, and vanilla and beat it well with an electric mixer, taking care to scrape the sides to make sure all of the cream cheese is beaten. Add the eggs a little bit at a time while beating the mixture until all the eggs are used. Slowly add the reserved strawberry mixture into the cream cheese mixture and beat until all is used. Spoon the mixture into the muffin pan. Place the muffin pan in a larger baking dish with a little water in the bottom and bake at 325 degrees for 25 minutes. After baking, remove the tins from the water and let them cool for 10 minutes before removing from the tins. Arrange on a serving platter or individual plates and serve. Serves 18.

Lagniappe: This is the real thing—cheesecake at its finest, but low-carb. Most of what's in a cheesecake is already low in carbs; it's the sugar that makes it a high-carb dish. Splenda® allows us to cook with an artificial sweetener that is just as good as sugar, but doesn't have anywhere near the carbs or calories. Enjoy!

Carbs per serving: 3.6 g.
Net carbs per serving: 3.1 g.
Calories per serving: 160

FRESH CHERRY SURPRISE

1 .3-oz package sugar-free gelatin, black cherry flavor

1 cup boiling water

1 8-oz. package cream cheese, softened and cut into squares

½ cup small curd cottage cheese (4 percent fat)

½ cup sour cream

½ cup fresh cherries, seeded and cut into small pieces

¼ cup pecans, chopped

¼ cup Splenda® sweetener

½ container Cool Whip® (4 oz.)

Put the gelatin in a small, metal bowl and pour the boiling water over it. Stir until the gelatin is completely dissolved. Add the cream cheese and stir until it begins to melt. Add the sour cream, cottage cheese, and cherries and stir until well mixed. Add the pecans and Splenda® and blend together well. Refrigerate for 30 minutes, covered until the gelatin starts to gel. Fold in the Cool Whip® and either put into individual serving glasses or bowl or put in one large bowl that you can serve out of with an ice cream scoop. Let the dish stand in the refrigerator for 3 hours then serve. Serves 8.

Lagniappe: I tried to decide if this was a salad or a dessert before I let the food testers decide. More thought it was a great dessert than thought it was a sweet salad, so here it is in the dessert section. There are limitless combinations you can make from this basic recipe. Using lemon gelatin and apples you can make Fresh Apple Surprise; using strawberry gelatin and fresh strawberries you can make Fresh Strawberry Surprise; and using blackberry gelatin and fresh blackberries you can make Fresh Blackberry Surprise. The list can go on and on. Use your imagination!

Carbs per serving: 7.2 g.
Net carbs per serving: 6.7 g.
Calories per serving: 222

PISTACHIO-STRAWBERRY TREAT

1 1-oz. package sugar-free instant
   pudding
2 cups half-and-half
½ cup sour cream
1 8-oz. package cream cheese,
   softened

½ 4-oz. container Cool Whip®, thawed
1 cup fresh strawberries, cut into
   about 6 pieces per berry
⅛ cup pecans, chopped

Mix together the pudding mix and the half-and-half with a hand mixer until well blended. Add the sour cream and blend in. Cut the cream cheese into 10 squares and drop them into the pudding mix. Beat together until all the cream cheese has blended into the pudding. Add the Cool Whip® and pecans and beat it in with the mixer until completely blended. Fold in the strawberries, taking care not to crush them. Pour into 6 individual serving bowls or cups. Refrigerate for 2 hours. Serve chilled. Serves 6.

Lagniappe: This is another quick and easy dessert that will please the discriminating dessert eater. You can do a lot of creative things with this dessert. Serve it as a parfait, layering the pudding mixture with fresh whipped cream until you get 3 or 4 layers and a dab of whipped cream on top. Add a few chopped nuts as a garnish. It really looks nice if you can find chopped pistachios. Or you can use half of a fresh strawberry on top. It makes for a delightful and beautiful dessert.

Carbs per serving: 11.1 g.
Net carbs per serving: 9.7 g.
Calories per serving: 304

COOKIE SUNDAY

1 low-carb chocolate cookie (2½ net carbs)

3 tbsp. whipped cream (sweetened with Splenda® sweetener)

½ cup low-carb ice cream (2 net carbs)

1 serving Chocolate Sauce (see p. 46 for the recipe)

1 tbsp. chopped almonds

Put the cookie on the bottom of a serving bowl. Cover the cookie with the ice cream. Put the Chocolate Sauce on top of the ice cream . Add the whipped cream and top with chopped almonds. Serve immediately. Serves 1.

Lagniappe: This is the dessert you need when everyone else is eating that big slice of chocolate cake. Your dessert will be bigger and everyone will want to have one too! This is quick and easy and you can keep all the ingredients around. I have stayed on this low-carb diet for over a year now, and one thing I've found out is that I couldn't do it if I couldn't have sweets! With this dessert, you don't give up anything. You are just making choices. Try adding fresh strawberries, too.

Carbs per serving: 30.5 g.
Net carbs per serving: 8.9 g.
Calories per serving: 462

BREAD PUDDING

8 slices of low-carb bread
2 cups half-and-half
½ stick unsalted butter, cut in to small pieces
4 eggs, slightly beaten
1½ cups Splenda® sweetener
1 tbsp. vanilla
½ cup fresh peaches, chopped
¾ cup raisins

1 Granny Smith apple, diced
½ cup pecans, chopped
1 tsp. allspice
1 tsp. nutmeg
1 tsp. cinnamon
butter to grease the bottom and sides of the baking pan
water to put into baking pan
1 recipe of Whiskey Sauce (see p. 45)

Preheat the oven to 350 degrees. Tear the bread into pieces and place in a large, glass bowl and set aside for later use. In a saucepan over low heat, combine the two creams and the butter. Heat over low heat until the butter is melted and the cream is hot. Pour this warm cream over the reserved bread and mix it together well. Let it stand for 10 minutes. Add the eggs, Splenda®, vanilla, peaches, raisins, and apple; blend together well. Add the spices and mix together well. Pour the mixture into a lightly-greased, ovenproof, 9 x 13-inch pan. Set this baking pan into a larger baking pan with 1-inch of water in it. Bake the pudding at 350 degrees for about 1 hour or until done. Check by inserting a knife into the center. If it comes out clean, then it's done. Allow the pudding to cool for 15 minutes before cutting. Serve hot or cold with whiskey, rum, brandy, or bourbon sauce. Serves 10.

Lagniappe: This bread pudding recipe is great right from the oven or reheated. If you refrigerate, it heats well in the microwave or you can heat it by placing it under the broiler for 2 minutes. It can also be frozen. Just defrost in the refrigerator until you are ready to serve. Be generous with the Whiskey Sauce; it compliments the pudding well.

Note: This recipe exceeds the Atkins' recommended use of Splenda®. However, the carb counts are accurate.

Carbs per serving: 23.6 g.
Net carbs per serving: 17.9 g.
Calories per serving: 428

Index